PUBLIC SPEAKING
——————THE——————
FREEMAN WAY

PUBLIC SPEAKING
———————THE———————
FREEMAN WAY

The Five Universal Laws of Public Speaking
I Learned from the Legendary
Dr. Thomas F. Freeman

PREVIN JONES

Published in the United States by:

CES Publishing

3353 Elgin Street

Houston, Texas 77004

Cover and interior design by Antonia Jones

ISBN: 978-0-615-52049-0

Library of Congress Control Number: 2011918174

Printed in the United States of America

TABLE OF CONTENTS

DEDICATION

This book is dedicated to my son Christian Gerald Jones, who was born premature weighing 1 pound 13 oz. By the grace of God and the great doctors and nurses at Texas Children's Hospital, Christian is now a healthy 2-year-old attending nursery school.

To God be the Glory!

Also, to my wife, Dawn Tezino Jones, thank you for your encouragement and support.

Previn Jones

INTRODUCTION

When I heard that Denzel Washington traveled to Houston, Texas, to meet with Dr. Thomas F. Freeman (Doc), the head coach of the Texas Southern University (TSU) Debate Team, I knew the two-time Academy Award winner searched for and selected the best debate coach in the country. Why did Denzel Washington take time out of his busy schedule to come all the way to Houston, Texas, to visit Dr. Freeman in his office on the campus of Texas Southern University? In preparation for the movie *The Great Debaters*, Denzel Washington and the cast sought the advice and consultation of Dr. Freeman and members of the TSU Debate Team to give them real insight into how ordinary students are transformed into extraordinary communicators. As a former student and mentee of Dr. Freeman, I always knew he was, and still is, one of the great communicators of our time. In fact, Dr. Freeman's body of work as a professor, debate coach, and minister spans from the industrial age of the twentieth century to the knowledge-based information age of the twenty-first century.

Public Speaking the Freeman Way was conceived out of my desire to honor Dr. Freeman by sharing with the world the ***Five Universal Laws*** of public speaking I learned from him as his student. This book should be considered a public speaking constitution that establishes the "rule of public speaking law." Simply stated, the purpose of this book is to establish a public speaking "constitutional framework" with specific guidelines, rules, principles, and applications that govern the discipline of public speaking. Similar to the constitution of our republic, which is the authoritative document that governs all branches of government, the principles and rules in this book govern all genres of public speaking.

No matter what type of presentation you are giving, this book is the authoritative document you should reference to ensure that your presentation is "constitutional." I was blessed and fortunate to learn these laws by observing the master speaker himself. Dr. Freeman and his internationally world-renowned debate team are best known, not only for producing great debaters, but also for developing great communicators. We were trained by one of the great masters of public speaking.

Those of you who don't know "Doc," as his students affectionately call him, may be curious as to why I call him a master. Dr. Freeman's extraordinary command of the English language and his mastery of both verbal and nonverbal communication have earned him a place in the public speakers' hall of fame.

One common attribute of all great orators, like the late Dr. Martin Luther King, Nelson Mandela, Dr. Thomas F. Freeman, and Presidents Bill Clinton and Barack Obama is that they know how to command the audience's attention and keep it! The late Congresswoman Barbara Jordan, who was a student of Dr. Freeman, demonstrated this ability when she captivated the nation at the 1976 National Democratic Convention with her mastery of the spoken word, coupled with her deep, hollowed baritone voice. Today, her speech is not only considered a great political convention speech, but it is also one of the great literary masterpieces of our time. It is well known that Congresswoman Barbara Jordan publicly credited and praised Dr. Freeman for helping her to develop and master her communication skills. Barbara said, "I thought I had superb diction and that no one would need to correct anything. Thomas Freeman found a flaw, and worked on it until it was corrected. I cannot overestimate the impact and influence Dr. Freeman had on my life."

While you may not be giving a nationally televised speech, you may be called upon to present a class project, deliver a local keynote address, deliver a business presentation, or speak at your local civic club meeting. Whatever the occasion, the universal laws taught in this book, if properly applied, will prepare you to be a great communicator. It is my expectation that after you study and apply the principles contained in this book, you will be able to prepare for and deliver a successful presentation one-hundred percent of the time.

WHY IS PUBLIC SPEAKING IMPORTANT?

"And the first place award goes to—Previn Jones from Texas Southern University!" As a freshman on the TSU Debate Team, I was stunned when I discovered that I had won my first international first place award at the 1996 International Debate and Forensics Competition in London, England. Many students participate on their debate teams while in college for four years and never win a first place award at the international level. It was surreal, and as I snapped out of my daze to step forward and accept my award, I just kept thinking to myself, "Everything Doc taught me really paid off in the end." In retrospect, I had no idea at the time how my training in public speaking from Dr. Freeman would help to shape my career after I turned my tassel and stepped into the real world.

From public figures to private citizens, knowing how to organize and articulate ideas effectively is a critical *life skill* that will add value to your life and give you a competitive advantage over those who are unaware of this truth. No matter what profession you decide to pursue, public speaking will more than likely require that you reach deep within yourself to articulate your thoughts in a structured manner. You may be a transactional attorney who does little public speaking, but your firm may request that you speak at a career day or try a pro bono case. You may be an environmental scientist who never has to speak in public, but the mayor of your city may ask your agency to give a presentation at a town hall meeting. You may be an entrepreneur who has a great idea and a business plan, but you are terrified by the thought of presenting to investors. You may be an introverted, straight "A" student who does not like to speak in class, but 60% of your final assignment is an oral presentation.

Whether your career, business venture, reputation, or scholastic grades are on the line, you simply can't hide anymore! It's time to overcome your self-imposed fear of public speaking and become a great communicator!

In the movie *The King's Speech*, Colin Firth portrays King George VI of England, who suffers from a debilitating speech impediment (stammer) that limits his ability to be an effective communicator. Hired by the King's wife, speech therapist Lionel Logue (Geoffrey Rush) tells the King in a heated argument that he is there to help him find his voice. I hope the lessons I learned from Dr. Freeman will help you find your voice. As my mentor, teacher, and friend, he helped me find mine.

DR. THOMAS FREEMAN

Distinguished Professor of Forensics at Texas Southern University
TSU Debate Team Coach since 1949
Minister of Mt. Horem Baptist Church since 1951

Dr. Thomas F. Freeman, Distinguished Professor of Forensics and Head Coach of the Texas Southern University Debate Team since 1949, has taught debate, speech and philosophy at TSU for more than half a century.

Dr. Freeman received a Bachelor of Arts from Virginia Newton University, Richmond, Virginia; a Bachelor of Divinity from Andover Newton Theological School, Newton Centre, Massachusetts; and a Doctor of Philosophy from the Divinity School of the University of Chicago, Chicago, Illinois. He engaged in postdoctoral studies at the University of Vienna, Austria, Vienna. Dr. Freeman pursued interinstitutional studies in 1973 at the Universities of Liberia, Lagos, and Ghana, and at Forbay College.

Dr. Freeman's talents as a spiritual leader are respected in both the higher education and the religious communities. Dr. Freeman has ministered at Pleasant St. Baptist Church in Westerly, Rhode Island; was Associate Minister of Monumental Baptist Church, Chicago, Illinois; and is presently Pastor of Mt. Horem Baptist Church, Houston, Texas, where he has provided spiritual guidance since 1951.

Named in his honor, the Thomas F. Freeman Center for Forensic Excellence at Texas Southern University develops students in the specialized techniques of effective oral communication through active participation in the forensic arts. It is also a showplace for the many awards the TSU

Debate Team has won in over 50 years of participation on the local, national, and international forensic circuits.

When asked why he continues to teach and coach after all these years, his response is: *"It's not about trophies and awards. It's the joy of seeing a young person evolve into greatness. That's what drives me."*

LAW I
MASTER YOUR MENTAL SELF

LAW I

MASTER YOUR MENTAL SELF

> *"Fear doesn't exist anywhere except in the mind."*
> **Dale Carnegie**
>
> *"Fear is the oldest and strongest emotion known to man, something deeply inscribed in our nervous system and subconscious...your fears are a kind of prison that confines you within a limited range of action. The less you fear, the more power you will have and the more fully you will live."*
> **Robert Greene**

LAW DEFINED

The process of purposefully influencing your belief system with positive and empowering thoughts to produce predetermined results of success.

PRINCIPLE
Know Thy Powerful Self

—————— SECTION 1 ——————
Rules of Mental Self-Mastery

RULE #1 — Win the Mental Battle First

As I mentioned in my introduction, Dr. Freeman possesses an extraordinary command of the English language and mastery of both verbal and nonverbal communication. Doc speaks to you with every fiber of his being—mind, body, soul, and spirit. I often say, *"You speak before you speak."* Doc's perfected ability to bring words to life with his colorful verbal and nonverbal expressions demonstrates just how well he has mastered his craft. When he walks onto a stage or into a room to deliver an address, he walks with the confidence of a commander preparing for the toughest theater of war. He walks with a confidence that says *"I know who I am and where I am going—follow me!"* No one will follow a commander into battle who is unsure and timid. As a communicator, you must remember this truth. Before you say one word, members of your audience are watching you. What are they looking for? CONFIDENCE

Dr. Freeman's confidence is so strong it emits a powerful aura that peaks the waiting audience's curiosity and interest. As you will learn in the laws to follow, your confidence emanates from a strong sense of personal purpose and the construct of your belief system.

However, I understand that this confidence does not come easily for some people and must be developed through proper training for those who fear public speaking. For some people, the fear of public speaking is akin to the fear of death; both fears consume the psyche and cause people to build an internal prison of self-containment, which limits their potential for greatness. This is what happened to King George VI in the movie the *King's Speech*. His own self-imposed fears were the source of his "stammer." This is why his speech therapist wanted to know who and what shaped his belief system as a child.

As a former debate coach and public relations consultant,

I have coached people from all walks of life who were absolutely terrified of the thought of public speaking. The fear of public speaking has infiltrated the minds (belief-systems) of many people from diverse backgrounds—black, white, rich, poor, learned, and unlearned. I don't care what country in the world you visit, you are sure to find someone who has a deathly fear of public speaking. How do we, once and for all, deal with this taunting, universal fear that has limited the potential of so many?

The answer is simple: you must first win the mental battle by being successful in your own mind first. This is the prerequisite for success in life and there is simply no way around it.

Let's go deeper.

RULE #2 — Develop an Empowered Belief System

The battle to conquer your fear of public speaking starts in the mind. As a former student of Dr. Freeman, who had the opportunity to learn directly from him, it is my belief that the source of his bold confidence and effectiveness is threefold:

1. He bases his thinking on an empowered belief system,
2. He is always prepared,
3. He perfects his craft through hard work and practice.

Thinking from an empowered belief system means you make decisions based on positive and empowering thoughts that serve as the construct of your belief system. Positive and empowering information means nothing if you don't believe it. Notice that I said *believe!* You can acquire a wealth of empowering information from books, seminars, audio/visual material, etc... but if you don't believe it, the results, or should I say lack of results, in your life will expose you. It is your responsibility to internalize and actually believe the positive and empowering information you put into your mind for it to manifest itself in the form of success. When you strongly believe something and have the action(s) to support the belief, your psychological disposition (mindset) will manifest itself in your experience. This is what I call the **Manifestation Principle.**

Let's explore this concept a little deeper. There are two complimentary schools of thought that explain this principle. From a biblical and philosophical perspective, the scriptures teach in **Proverbs 23:7** that *"as a man thinketh in his heart, so is he."* Famous philosopher Rene

Descartes reiterated this principle when he said, *"I think, therefore I am."* Implied in this perspective is the notion that the person you are and the person you are becoming are simply "manifestations" of your thoughts. Let me put it this way: you will see your conscious and subconscious thoughts every day in your decisions, actions, and habits. From a scientific perspective, quantum physics contends that thought and matter are different manifestations of the same substance—Energy. For those who don't know, quantum physics is the study of how the world works on the smallest scale, at a level far smaller than the atom, which is called the subatomic level.[1]

My intent is not to go into detail about the discipline of quantum physics but to point out the power and capacity of the human belief system to produce tangible results. The science of quantum physics hypothesizes that *thought influences matter.* This hypothesis is based on the rationale that everything is energy, and your thoughts can influence that energy. For example, if you go to any major city in America, you will see majestic skyscrapers kissing the skyline in a vertical direction, reaching toward the earth's stratosphere. Stop for a moment and realize that these majestic architectural feats, made from thousands of tons of steel, were once just a thought in someone's mind. From the Empire State Building in New York to the Eiffel Tower in Paris, France, to the tallest building in the world—Dubai's Burj Khalifa (2,717 ft.), it is a fact that these structures were all simply thoughts in someone's mind and were manifested into tangible structures of matter through the power of thought influence and hard work.

All of these grand structures have one thing in common—**thought preceded the thing. My point is this: thought**

was the genesis or origin of their existence. The house you live in, the car you drive, and the company you work for were all just thoughts in someone's mind before they were manifested as tangible realities. Therefore, it can be concluded that thoughts can produce tangible results that can be directly linked to the genesis of specific ideas. This is why you cannot let your thoughts run wild. You must take authority over your thoughts by developing an empowered belief system that will serve as the origin and basis for all your decisions. You must once and for all cancel this horrific reality show of defeat that keeps playing in your mind called "thoughts gone wild." It's time to change the channel, and get control of your thoughts.

As a student of Doc, I not only learned public speaking principles and techniques, but I also learned a far more valuable life skill that still serves me well to this day— making decisions from an empowered belief system.

LAW IN ACTION

I firmly believe that Doc's faith influences his empowered belief system. This can be seen in his decision-making process and the way he lives his life. When I joined the team, I remember a senior student telling me about an incident that demonstrated Doc's empowered belief system in action. The students were scheduled to drive to an out-of-state competition to compete in one of many scheduled intercollegiate debate tournaments. However, the National Weather Service issued a severe thunderstorm watch, and university officials decided not to sponsor the trip. Doc decided he would continue his scheduled trip, and any student who wanted to attend could still go at his or her own risk. Doc utilized his personal vehicle and led the students safely to the tournament and a first-place place victory for Texas Southern University. Some may say Doc's decision was disingenuous and put the students in harm's way. However, collegiate debaters are adults and can make their own decisions. Secondly, Doc's belief system, which stems from his personal faith, gave him peace of mind and confidence that his God would take care of him and his students. Many Christians, Muslims, and Jews (or whatever your religious persuasion is), tend to conveniently leave their faith at church, the mosque, or synagogue.

What is my point?

Doc's bold confidence and fearlessness in public speaking is a manifestation of his empowered belief system, which is rooted in his faith. Your personal faith is a great starting point to develop and cultivate an empowered belief system that will serve as the origin and genesis of your confidence and decision-making process.

The Torah, the Bible, and the Koran are filled with examples of great men and women who overcame their fears through an empowered belief system rooted in their faith. To drive this point home, I want to be clear: **don't leave your faith at home when you have a speaking engagement!** Stop being afraid of confronting your fears! It is your responsibility to put your personal faith in action to overcome both internal and external obstacles to achieve victory.

Case Example: Rudy

Another example of how "Winning the Mental Battle" can lead to desired results is the story of Rudy. We all remember the 1993 hit movie *Rudy* about the life of Daniel "Rudy" Ruettiger. This true story provides a vivid account of Rudy's journey to become a Notre Dame football player in spite of the insurmountable obstacles he faced. What were those obstacles? First, he didn't have the grades to get into Notre Dame. Second, he didn't have the financial means. Third, he didn't have the athletic ability or physical size of most Notre Dame recruits. Fourth, he received his fair share of discouragement from close friends and family who simply said it was impossible. However, Rudy had something that overcame all of his obstacles—**an empowered belief system rooted in a strong sense of purpose.** Rudy's belief that he would one day attend Notre Dame and play football was so strong and definite that it manifested itself in every aspect of his life. His work ethic on and off the field was evidence that he was winning the mental battle, even though others could not see it. Although he had several setbacks and disappointments on and off the field, his resolve never wavered because *his empowered belief system was the foundation for his confidence.* Rudy ended up being accepted to Notre Dame and became a member of their famous football team. Rudy now travels the country speaking and telling his story.

You may not be facing insurmountable obstacles like Rudy, but you, too, can develop the same tenacious resolve to overcome your fear of public speaking. Fear is an outgrowth of disabling, negative thought(s). Most people think their beliefs are secret; however, we must realize that all of our actions are manifestations of what we believe. Consider the student who fakes being sick to miss school because he is afraid of giving an oral presentation. Or the executive who is visibly nervous as he trembles, stumbles over words, and sweats constantly during a major presentation. The actions—faking being sick, trembling, stumbling over words, and sweating—are all outward manifestations of internal disabling beliefs, not only about public speaking but about "what you believe."

Rule #3 — Understand Your Belief System Breakdown

Most disabling beliefs come from poor self-concept beliefs that are steeped in fear—I'm unattractive; I'm fat; I'm not smart enough; I don't belong here, etc. You may think these beliefs are safe and secure in the secret chambers of your mind, but I can assure you that they will disclose themselves in the most embarrassing ways.

Your belief system is the basis for your way of thinking, and your way of thinking is the basis for your actions. Consider the belief system diagram below.

Belief-System Diagram

Your belief system is the systematic organization of ideas that produce consistent results of failure or success. The bottom line is this: either you will think from a **failure-based belief system**, which is rooted in fear, or you will think from a **success-based belief system** that is rooted in positive, empowered thinking. Let's explore the aforementioned belief systems further.

Example: Failure-Based Belief System

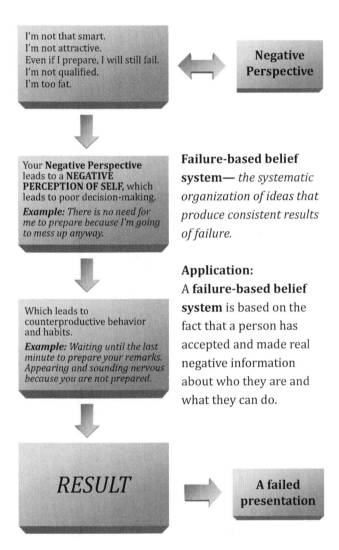

I'm not that smart.
I'm not attractive.
Even if I prepare, I will still fail.
I'm not qualified.
I'm too fat.

Negative Perspective

Your **Negative Perspective** leads to a **NEGATIVE PERCEPTION OF SELF,** which leads to poor decision-making.
Example: There is no need for me to prepare because I'm going to mess up anyway.

Which leads to counterproductive behavior and habits.
Example: Waiting until the last minute to prepare your remarks. Appearing and sounding nervous because you are not prepared.

RESULT

A failed presentation

Failure-based belief system— *the systematic organization of ideas that produce consistent results of failure.*

Application:
A **failure-based belief system** is based on the fact that a person has accepted and made real negative information about who they are and what they can do.

Example: Success-Based Belief System

I know who I am and what I want.
I am attractive because I say I am.
I must prepare in order to be successful.
I have the potential to be whatever I want to be.
I am a great public speaker and communicator.

Positive Perspective

Your **Positive Perspective** leads to an **EMPOWERED PERCEPTION OF SELF.**
Example: Oprah Winfrey said, *"I always believed I would be great."*

Success-based belief system— *the systematic organization of ideas that produce consistent results of success.*

Which leads to empowered decision-making.
Example: I must study and work hard if I am going to live up to my potential. I must prepare relentlessly in order to communicate an effective message.

Application:
A **success-based belief system** is based on the fact that a person has accepted and made real positive and empowering information about who they are and what they can do.

Which leads to productive behavior and habits.
Example: Planning for success through disciplined, focused, and goal-oriented preparation.

RESULT

A successful presentation

My purpose for meticulously demonstrating how a belief system produces results of failure or success is to sear into your consciousness YOUR responsibility to daily develop and guard your belief system. You must prepare for and own your success, and it starts by focusing your thoughts.

Don't let fear become your focus

Identifying and knowing how to overcome self-imposed fears that are handicapping you from being your best is a critical first step. With the advent of social media platforms like Facebook and Twitter, we have digital access to a reservoir of people's thoughts, ideas, and fears, which gives us direct insight into why people believe what they believe. I posted this question on my Facebook page: why do most people fear public speaking? Below are some of the comments I received.

Comment 1
REJECTION is one reason why some people fear public speaking....

Comment 2
Feeling self-conscious about something, and worried that being in front of people magnifies a perceived flaw...

Comment 3
Fear of the unknown. Fear that we will not be able to fulfill the expectations of those in the audience.

Comment 4
Apprehension over being JUDGED! When we are speaking in front of an audience we KNOW that others are hanging onto our every word. Most people worry so much about HOW they are articulating particular words that the passion for what they are conveying becomes obsolete. Therefore, they begin to think too hard and mess up...

Comment 5
It's the FEAR of being judged...

The common theme that seems to weave its way through all of the comments is the FEAR of being judged. This fear is based on what I call **negative self-consciousness**, which stems from your belief system. Negative self-consciousness is defined as the adopted belief of your perceived internal and external negative perceptions of self. Having a disempowering, **failure-based belief system** not only negatively affects your thinking but also your consciousness of who you are and what you can do. There are both internal and external barriers that play major roles in shaping a person's **negative self-consciousness**. The **internal barriers** are based on negative, self-imposed thoughts. If you say to yourself, I don't want to speak before all those people because I'm overweight, and everyone will look at me and see how fat I am, then you direct your FOCUS and attention to your weight—not the presentation. If you say to yourself repeatedly, I'm afraid of freezing and stumbling, then you focus your attention on freezing and stumbling—not the presentation. If you say to yourself, who am I to speak to such a prestigious audience, then you are essentially focusing on the belief that the people in the audience are somehow better than you—not the presentation. Below are the three most dangerous internal barriers you must avoid:

1. Low-self esteem.
2. Self-hatred.
3. An "Inferiority complex".

The **external barriers** that cause **negative self-consciousness** are based on the fact that you have allowed other people's negative opinions about you to become your own. Never take ownership of someone else's negativity. This is especially true for young, impressionable students. If another student calls you stupid and dumb and you believe it, this will become your focus. For professionals, if your coworker tells you that you are just not smart enough to do this job—don't believe it! The moment you do, you have conceded your most powerful personal attribute— the ability to define yourself. Below are the three most dangerous external barriers you must avoid:

1. Giving someone the power to define you in negative terms.
2. Believing negative opinions of others.
3. Making decisions based on those negative opinions.

LAW IN ACTION

I remember a young student by the name of Jonathan who attended one of my summer public-speaking workshops. He was absolutely terrified to speak before the class because the other kids teased him about a slight speech impediment. The other kids called him *"retarded man."* One day I asked him why he never paid attention in class. He said, *"I'm retarded, and I can't learn this stuff."* Because he allowed external negative information to shape his view of himself, he developed a negative perception of who he was and what he could do, which led to a defeatist attitude. Again, never own someone else's negative view of who you are. You must NEVER concede your power to define yourself. I began to work with Jonathan by reprogramming him to believe that he was just as smart as, and even smarter than, the other kids who teased him. I told him that his brain just processed information faster than his mouth could produce words. I taught him how to slow down and annunciate his words more carefully. I also taught him some positive affirmations, which I discuss later in the book, so that he could focus his thoughts and boost his self-esteem. The result was that, at the conclusion of the workshop, Jonathan delivered a stunning presentation that commanded a standing ovation, even from those who had previously teased him. The problem was not the speech impediment but the external and internal negative barriers Jonathan chose to focus on. Focus is so powerful that you literally become what you focus on.

For example, if you focus on law for three years in law school, then you can become a lawyer. If you focus on medicine in medical school, then you can become a doctor. If you focus on social work, then you can become a social worker. If you focus on doubt, then you become a doubter. If you focus on a poor image of self, then you become that poor self-image. If you focus on failure, then you become a FAILURE. Focusing on disempowering beliefs and emotions, such as self-doubt, fear, and anxiety, will produce doubtful, fearful, and timid behavior. I understand that new racecar drivers are taught not to focus on the wall if they lose control of the car. Why? Because focusing on the wall will more than likely lead them in that direction, resulting in a deadly crash. Don't focus on the wall of fear and doubt. You must train your mind to focus on positive and empowering beliefs, such as positive self worth, love of self, love of others, self-respect, self-validation, personal confidence, etc.

RULE #4 — Develop a Positive
Self-Consciousness through Proper Focus

Focus is a powerful tool that can help you willfully and purposefully direct your thoughts. If a photographer wants to snap a clear picture, he must focus his lens first. If you want a clear, positive picture of yourself, you must focus your internal lens, which is your self-consciousness. As I mentioned earlier, you decide what type (negative or positive) of information you believe about yourself. Your internal lens of self-consciousness can focus on pictures of negative images (thoughts) of yourself or pictures of positive images (thoughts) of yourself. The one thing you need to be absolutely clear about is that you have the power to form a clear picture of how you define yourself by what you focus on. If you ALLOW internal and external negative self-conscious thoughts to become your focus, the mental picture you will have of yourself will be clear: LOSER, STUPID, FAT, DUMB, FAILURE etc.

Thoughts are like seeds; their purpose is to produce exponentially the substance that's on the inside of the seed. When I showed Jonathan his self-worth by explaining he was super intelligent because his brain processes information so fast that his mouth couldn't keep up, I was tilling the ground of his mind so that I could plant seeds of success to refocus his thoughts. I implore you to focus on empowering beliefs that will focus your thoughts to manifest the greatness that's within you.

RULE #5 — **Affirm Yourself**

The Psychology of Confidence
Lack of self-confidence stems from various causal factors. The chief causal factor is misguided focus. Stop taking ownership of and focusing on others' negative beliefs of you, and get rid of your own negative thoughts.

LAW IN ACTION

Your perception of yourself should always come from a positive context. I teach this to my students in public speaking workshops because I say it to myself: I am somebody, I have something to say, and the world needs to hear it!

Say it right now.

I am somebody, I have something to say, and the world needs to hear it!

I am somebody, I have something to say, and my class needs to hear it!

I am somebody, I have something to say, and the board needs to hear it!

I am somebody, I have something to say, and city council needs to hear it!

I am somebody, I have something to say, and the jury/ judge needs to hear it!

I am somebody, I have something to say, and the church needs to hear it!

Positive and authoratative affirmations that you BELIEVE will help to cultivate a **positive self-consciousness** by focusing and directing your internal thoughts of self with empowering, uplifting information that builds self-confidence. You must re-program your mind with positive information that will serve as the basis for your positive focus. Consider the affirmations listed below, which you can say to yourself every day until you start believing them.

1. *I am a man/woman of purpose and vision!*
2. *I am a man/woman of excellence!*
3. *I am a great communicator!*
4. *I am a person with great gifts and talents that I must share with the world!*
5. *My presentation will be successful and effective!*
6. *My presentation will inspire, motivate, and move people to action!*

Programming your mind with positive affirmations to direct your focus is the first step in tearing down the mental and psychological walls of self-doubt and fear. I used this method with Jonathan, as well as many of my students (both adult and adolescents).

RULE #6 — Plant Seeds of Success

Positive and empowering affirmations are the seeds of success that must be planted by you. Your mind is fertile and will yield back to you in great measure what you put (plant) in it. James Allen put it best in his critically acclaimed essay, *"As a Man Thinketh."*

Excerpt:
The aphorism, "As a man thinketh in his heart so is he," not only embraces the whole of a man's being, but is so comprehensive as to reach out to every condition and circumstance of his life. A man is literally what he thinks, his character being the complete sum of all his thoughts.

As the plant springs from, and could not be without, the seed, so every act of a man springs from the hidden seed of thought, and could not have appeared without them.

Consider the concept of farming. If a farmer wants to reap a harvest of mustard greens, he must plant mustard seeds in fertile soil. This is a law of nature as well as a mental law. You can't plant mustard seeds and expect carrots to grow, just like you can't expect a successful presentation if you constantly plant thoughts (seeds) of failure in your mind. It's simple: if you want mustards, you must plant mustard seeds. If you want a successful presentation, you must plant successful thoughts on a daily basis, not just prior to the presentation. It's a lifestyle. When you plant seeds in the ground, the seeds will go through the germination process and give back to the farmer that which was already in the seed. Mustard seeds are about one-sixteenth of an inch in diameter but can produce an abundance of mustard greens, weighing thousands of pounds. Filling your mind with empowering, positive thought seeds will yield back to you that which is already in you—a multitude of SUCCESS.

In retrospect, when I think about the seeds of excellence and belief in one's ability that Doc planted in us as students, I understand why he demanded so much of us. His desire was that all of his students not only become effective communicators but also excel beyond the university experience and use our skills to make a difference. Because he planted positive affirmations (seeds) in his students' minds by telling us we were the best, many of his students are now using the skills we learned on his debate team in academia, politics, business, entertainment, law, and medicine. As young impressionable college students, Doc told us we were great, and we believed him! As a result, we won several first place awards, both nationally and internationally. You must tell yourself and believe that you can and will be a great communicator. There are some very powerful contemporary examples of the power of how belief can translate into success.

LAW IN ACTION

For example, Oprah Winfrey said in an interview on Barbara Walters' annual Oscar special, *"I always believed I would be great."* Oftentimes we see people of great success but don't understand the source of their success. Oprah was essentially saying that greatness starts out as a seed in your belief system. I implore you to develop your own positive affirmations of greatness and internalize them through repetition, focus, and hard work. It's your responsibility to plant your own seeds of success by **Mastering Your Mental Self.**

Some of you who are reading this book may ask, "Why dedicate so much time and space to the concept of mental mastery?" As an experienced speaking consultant, I have learned that I can teach specific public speaking skills and techniques for a successful presentation, but if a person is terrified with fear, then that person will forget everything I taught him or her. Your confidence and stage presence will emanate from your belief system and a strong sense of personal purpose. Public speaking law declares that if you want to be a successful public speaker, then you must: **MASTER YOUR MENTAL SELF.**

LAW II
DISCIPLINED PREPARATION

LAW II

DISCIPLINED PREPARATION

> *"When preparation and opportunity meet in the womb of time it gives birth to greatness."*
> **Unknown**

LAW DEFINED

The process of focusing your research to accomplish time-specific goals and objectives for a specific project.

PRINCIPLE
Fail to Plan, Plan to Fail

SECTION I
Lessons from the Navy SEALs

Now that you BELIEVE you can be a great communicator and have developed your confidence level, it is time to prepare yourself with disciplined psychological and physical training that will prepare you for the battlefield of actually speaking in public.

Many of you know, from the movie *GI Jane,* that Navy SEALs undergo rigorous physical and psychological training to prepare them to function in extremely stressful situations. At the Navy SEALs Special Warfare Command Center in San Diego, recruits are put through specialized training to change the way they react to fear. The objective of this

39

type of training is to teach recruits how to suppress their self-imposed fear, which could get them killed in the field. Navy SEALs must know how to perform and exercise their best judgment under extreme life and death situations. So, how do the Navy SEALs' instructors prepare their recruits for success? Recruits are introduced to various chaotic situations that will increase their capacity to control their fear impulses, which gives them the ability to think rationally and function at the highest level, even while under attack. According to neuroscience researchers, "When confronted with what the brain perceives as fear, it's the amygdala (central command center for processing emotions) that responds to information from our senses. The senses are sent through the brain stem to the body, causing nervousness, sweating, and anxiety."[1]

The purpose of introducing the Navy SEAL recruits to chaotic situations in a controlled environment is to reconfigure how the brain processes and reacts to perceived "fearful" situations. The most intensive training exercise is the **Underwater Pool Competency Test** which requires recruits to spend at least twenty minutes underwater while experiencing constant violent attacks on their breathing equipment from their instructors.

Note: Prior to this test, recruits are prepared with systematic instructions on how to repair their water equipment if disabled. During the **Underwater Pool Competency Test,** several experienced instructors accompany their recruit to a large pool for the purpose of mounting a consistent, vigorous attack on their breathing equipment while the recruits are underwater. The recruits must quickly repair their equipment and stay underwater for a full twenty minutes without coming up. The fear of not being able to breathe causes intense stress and panic, which is why this extreme training is used to psychologically prepare Navy SEALs to stay calm in stressful situations. Each recruit, in the split second between being attacked and the natural reaction of the brain to panic, has to make a decisive decision—do I panic and rise for air or stay calm and repair my air hose as I was trained? Many recruits fail this portion of the training, but the ones who prevail will advance to the next stage of fulfilling their requirements to become a Navy SEAL.

LAW IN PRACTICE

What if you are under psychological attack by your fear of public speaking? You must, through disciplined preparation, constructive criticism, and rigorous training, reconfigure how you react when you are under attack by your own self-destructive thinking and behavior.

At this particular point in your training, you don't need to know the mechanics of public speaking, but you need to know how to conquer fear, overcome anxiety, and function at the highest level under pressure. The Navy SEALs instructors use four universal techniques to help their recruits focus their thoughts.

1. GOAL-SETTING

Goal-setting will help you properly organize information by engaging the frontal lobe of the brain. The front part of the brain is where planning, organizing, problem solving, selective attention, and a variety of "higher cognitive functions," including behavior and emotions, occur.[2] By goal setting, we force our minds to focus on achieving a desired result within a specific timeframe. Navy SEALs are taught to plan their moves several steps ahead to achieve specific objectives within the context of their mission. **Your mission is to deliver the right message to the right audience at the right time,** which starts in the preparation stage. One tool available to help you put things in perspective and organize your research with time-specific benchmarks is the **Speech Goal-Setting Plan.** The Speech Goal-Setting Plan is the process of establishing time-specific, goal-oriented benchmarks to measure your pre-speech preparation progress.

See Speech Goal-Setting Plan example on next page.

Sample Goal-Setting Plan

Mission Clarity - Deliver the right message to the right audience at the right time.

Goal I - Identify the demographics and expertise of your prospective audience.

Goal II - Get clarity from the event organizers regarding their expectations of you as a speaker.

Goal III - Prepare a presentation appropriate for the audience within the time constraint allotted to you.

Goal IV - Perfect your presentation with constructive criticism and evaluation prior to the event.

Execution Plan

I. Send speaker's request form and survey to event organizers by January 1. *(I will go into more detail about the importance of the speaker's request form and survey later in this chapter.)* **Note:** Be time-specific and let the organizers know you must have the information by a certain date in order to properly prepare for the event.

II. Receive and analyze speaker's request form by January 15. **Note:** Before you begin the preparation process for your presentation, you must know exactly who your audience is and what they expect of you.

III. Select topic, conduct research, and draft outline by February 1. **Note:** Your research timeframe will be contingent upon various factors: date of presentation, expertise, complexity of material etc.

IV. Finish first speech draft and begin practice February 5. **Note:** If you are using the manuscript method, which means you actually write out the entire speech word-for-word, you should begin writing as soon as you are satisfied with your outline.

V. Get feedback through simulation. **Note:** You may ask family, friends, and co-workers to evaluate your presentation and give you constructive criticism to help you improve.

VI. Have an on-site dress rehearsal. **Note:** If possible, go to the actual venue to practice. This will familiarize you with the actual environment and remove some of the anxiety associated with the unknown.

This document is essentially your war plan. As any good military general will tell you, you must understand every aspect of an operation and plan for the unexpected if you are going to be victorious in war. Goal-setting is a critical life skill that overlaps every aspect of your life. Whether it's your personal life, school, or work, you must establish benchmarks to measure your progress. By establishing time-specific, goal-oriented benchmarks, you can monitor and quantify your progress with measureable metrics.

For example, setting a goal to have the first outline and draft of your speech completed one month before the speaking engagement so that you can practice more on your delivery will focus your attention on accomplishing a desired result within a specific timeframe. If you set a goal to practice your presentation before family, friends, or a focus group two weeks in advance to process feedback and make adjustments, you are again focusing your attention for a specific, time-sensitive result. By utilizing this technique, you will avoid the number one contributor to poor presentations—procrastination. Because most people don't like public speaking, they will put off the preparation process as long as possible so that they don't have to think about it because thinking about it stirs up negative emotions and feelings. **Therefore, developing time-specific benchmarks in the form of goals and objectives to manage your time and focus your preparation is a key component of the application of the law of Disciplined Preparation.** Use your time wisely to accomplish small victories. Goal setting will not work if you don't have the discipline to follow through. Writing down goals on paper is useless if you don't bring them to life with subsequent action.

2. VISUALIZATION *(Seeing is Believing!)*

Some people simply don't believe something until they see it. Well, visualization allows you to see yourself being successful. There is no other way to say it; you must see your own success first!

Visualization allows you to go over the activity in your mind (so when you are faced with the situation, it won't be your first time). Visualization gives you the power to create in your mind a picture of your future success. When I heard that billionaire Oprah Winfrey uses a vision board, I said that there must really be something to this concept. Why do I make such a statement? After building a multibillion dollar media empire from nothing, I think she is qualified to be a point of reference that visualization is a viable strategy to achieve results.

You must see yourself delivering a great presentation to an attentive audience. Keep in mind that visualization does not mean you can bypass the hard work of preparation and practice. Visualization simply allows you to see in advance the fruit of your hard work and preparation. You can visualize beautiful mustard greens all day, but you still have to cultivate the ground, plant the seeds, water them, keep out the weeds, and harvest your crop. Great communicators use a similar work ethic to prepare their presentations.

Cultivating the ground
Application: It is your responsibility to get all of the pertinent information about the audience and the context of the event from the speaker's request (survey) form.

Planting seeds of success
Application: You must believe that disciplined preparation will help you prepare and deliver a great presentation.

Watering your seeds
Application: You must speak positive affirmations to yourself to grow your confidence.

Keeping out the weeds
Application: It is your responsibility to pluck negative thoughts from your mental garden of success.

Harvesting
Application: It's finally time for you to deliver your perfected presentation with bold confidence.

Visualization gives you the power to be successful where it counts the most—in your own mind. Many of us play a failed presentation repeatedly in our minds because of our fear of public speaking. No wonder you are scared to death of public speaking. You keep playing the same horror movie of you failing in your mind. Your inner beliefs and thoughts will set the stage for the movie you will star in, direct, and produce. This is why you must consistently see yourself being successful. To those who think visualization is some intangible concept that does not produce results, consider the following example.

Legendary baseball player Willie Mayes said in an interview with Tavis Smiley that he would see, in dreams, the things he did on the baseball field prior to them happening. If you are not familiar with the success of Willie Mayes' career, I implore you to Google him or buy the book, *Willie Mayes: The Life, The Legend* by James S. Hirsch.

3. SELF-TALK

Self-talk is another technique the Navy SEALs use to focus their thoughts. Brain experts contend that the average person speaks to himself 300-1000 words per minute.[3] You must feed your subconscious mind positive, reassuring affirmations that you can and will deliver an effective presentation. Positive thoughts of success will reinforce your visualization of success, which prepares the brain to override your fear of public speaking. Knowing in advance that your presentation will be successful is not being arrogant, but it is a mental prerequisite for a successful delivery. **Remember:** your preparation for a speech starts before you begin to research and write the speech. You must condition yourself to see it. Believe it. Do it. You must be your biggest fan! Cheer yourself on!

4. AROUSAL CONTROL

Arousal control deals with proper breathing techniques to relax the body. For example, a long exhale mimics the body's relaxation process by sending more oxygen to the brain.[4] Taking deep breaths through your nose and exhaling through your mouth helps to relax your body. Some people are so terrified of public speaking that they actually hyperventilate, which causes the body to lose excessive amounts of carbon dioxide. This loss of carbon dioxide triggers symptoms such as gasping, trembling, choking, and the feeling of being smothered. Knowing how to consciously engage in "slow, deep diaphragmatic breathing is recommended" to remedy this problem.[5] Breathing techniques learned in yoga are excellent ways to develop your breathing skills. Many experts consider breathing techniques taught in yoga as an intermediary between the mind and body. Your body should be the servant of the mind. Practicing proper breathing techniques gives you a tool to alter your physiological state at will. To learn more about breathing techniques, you may start by researching the following references.

Gallego, J., Nsegbe, E., and Durand, E. (2001). Learning in respiratory control. *Behavior Modification, 25* (4), 495-512.

Guz, A., (1997). Brain, breathing and breathlessness. *Respiration Physiology.* (1997).

Jerath, R., Edry, J. W, Barnes, V.A., and Jerath, V. (2006). Physiology of long pranayamic breathing: Neural respiratory elements may provide a mechanism that explains how slow deep breathing shifts the autonomic nervous system. *Medical Hypothesis.*

Pal, G.K., Velkumary, S., and Madanmohan. (2004). Effect of short-term practice of breathing exercises on autonomic functions in normal human volunteers. *Indian Journal of Medical Research.*

Repich, D. (2002). *Overcoming concerns about breathing.* National Institute of Anxiety and Stress, Inc.

I would like to add a fifth technique to help you focus your preparation for success—experience.

5. EXPERIENCE

Nothing will compensate for the competency and confidence you gain from actual experience. The more you engage in public speaking the less you will be afraid of it. In fact, just like the Navy SEALs, you should use rigorous simulated and actual situations to help you develop your proficiency in public speaking. As you are learning the laws of success in public speaking, you must put them to work in a practical way. Practicing in a simulated environment is a great way to overcome your fears, develop your skills, and build confidence prior to your engagement.

SIMULATION

Simulated training can be done in a controlled environment with a focus group of family, friends, or strangers. You want tough but fair critics who will give you constructive criticism. Dr. Freeman uses this method with his debate team. As a freshman on the team, I found myself debating and speaking before senior members of the team who didn't bite their tongues. If your presentation was horrible, they told you so and then gave you constructive critiques to help you improve. Just as the Navy SEALs undergo vigorous attacks during the Underwater Pool Competency Test, simulated public speaking training should be designed to be rigid and tough for the purpose of improving your skills.

One senior member on the team told me, "Hey man, we are hard on you because we don't want you to go to competition and embarrass yourself and the university. We want you to be the best. Hey, somebody has to take my place when I'm gone." By making my mistakes and having them corrected in a simulated environment, I was confident and competent

49

when it came time to actually compete in intercollegiate competition. If you have a class presentation due at school, let your parents or peers hear it first. Give them the same criteria your teacher will use to grade the assignment. I can assure you that the feedback you get will be invaluable and will make the difference between receiving an A or C as your grade.

As members of Doc's debate team, we also used impromtu speaking to overcome anxiety and develop public speaking proficiency. Impromptu speaking within the context of intercollegiate competition requires you to develop three to four points on a topic and elaborate on those points in a specified amount of time before a judge. Students are given a limited amount of time, called "prep time," to organize their thoughts. After prep time, the judge assesses your ability to give a relevant and coherent presentation with distinguishing points on the selected topic. This method of training helps you develop proficiency in organizing your thoughts and thinking quickly on your feet. You can practice this skill with close family, friends, and coworkers.

Here is an example of an impromptu speech outline based on a quote by Barbara Jordan: *"What the people want is simple—they want an America as good as its promise."* Barbara Jordan

Introduction:
The eloquence of the late Congresswoman Barbara Jordan still holds true today: *"What the people want is simple— they want an America as good as its promise."* What is the promise of America? That all would have the right to life, liberty, and the pursuit of happiness. What is the promise of America? That in order to form a more perfect union we

hold these truths to be self-evident that all men are created equal. As a representative of the people, Barbara Jordan was simply holding America accountable to the principles inherently imbedded in the freedom document we call the Constitution—freedom, justice, and equality. If we are going to be the great nation that America was envisioned to be, we must uphold the principles of Freedom, Justice and Equality in our most sacred democratic institutions—the executive, legislative, and judicial branches of government.

Point 1: Freedom, justice, and equality must be the guiding principles of our chief executive—the President of the United States. (Elaborate)

Point 2: Freedom, justice, and equality must be the guiding principles of our members of Congress. (Elaborate)

Point 3: Freedom, justice, and equality must be the guiding principles of our interpreters of the law—the United States Supreme Court. (Elaborate)

Note: The point of impromptu speaking is to organize your thoughts about a specific topic in a limited amount of time (5-7 minutes) to further explain its substance by using coordinated points for elaboration. I simply took Barbara Jordan's quote about America's promise and focused it on the three most important democratic institutions of government. My objective was to ensure that the judge or audience clearly understood that Barbara Jordan's theme of accountability is applicable to all branches of government.

The more you practice impromptu speaking before others, the more proficient you will become in organizing your thoughts and overcoming your fear of public speaking. After several practice sessions with my fellow debate colleagues and actually utilizing this skill in competition, I developed an extraordinary proficiency for clearly organizing and articulating my thoughts, especially when I had sufficient time to prepare. It's similar to the repetitive drills that football, basketball, and baseball players go through in practice to prepare for game day.

Within the context of public speaking, game day is actually speaking in a public setting. Getting actual experience by speaking in public forums like church services, civic club meetings, in class, or for special work assignments before accepting a keynote speaking engagement is invaluable. This will give you an opportunity to overcome the real pressures and anxieties you may have when it comes to public speaking. The idea is to experience small victories that will help you overcome those perceived pressures and anxieties. Little victories lead to big victories, and big victories lead to you becoming a great communicator. You should also ask friends and co-workers to constructively critique your major presentations before the event. It's a good idea to have your own focus group in order to get feedback and constructive criticism on a small scale before you go public. Also, I highly encourage students to join their school's debate team, which teaches advanced speech and debate skills. This will give you a competitive advantage over your peers, especially when no one wants to volunteer to be the representative who presents the class project. You will be the leader.

To those who fear public speaking, speaking before an audience may be equivalent to the Navy SEALs' recruit having his breathing equipment attacked underwater. Just remember—the more training and small victories you have, the more confident you will be when you have to give that big presentation at work or deliver a major keynote address.

I remember one student in particular who made excellent grades but was horrified of public speaking. Her mother recommended that she join the debate team to overcome her fear of public speaking. She would literally tremble when it was her time to speak during practice. After a month of rigorous practice and constant constructive critiques, I began to see her confidence and speaking proficiency blossom. She began volunteering during drills and workshops. After several months of practice and actual experience in competition, she became an award-winning debater and poetic speaker. With the proper training and experience, you, too, can become an excellent communicator.

──────── SECTION II ────────
Know Your Audience

PRINCIPLE
You Must Know Who, in Order to Know Why.

Before you begin to brainstorm, outline your presentation, and write your masterpiece, ask yourself a critical question: To whom am I speaking to and why? Disciplined preparation requires you to strategically research and gather information about your audience in order to focus and guide the preparation and delivery process. I call this *audience-focused preparation*.

LAW IN ACTION

I know you want to jump right in and write a great speech, but your masterpiece may be all wrong for the audience you are speaking to. It is possible to have the right message for the wrong audience. For example, I received an invitation to speak to an organization that teaches adult literacy classes in underprivileged communities with high levels of adult illiteracy. The invitation did not specify who the target audience would be. On the surface, I assumed I would be speaking to the adult students who were receiving the literacy training. However, after I called and questioned the person who invited me, I discovered that I would be speaking to the volunteers who teach the literacy classes. The volunteers are professionals—lawyers, doctors, teachers, and business executives from the community who volunteer their time to help reduce adult illiteracy in Houston.

Before I made the call, I had painted a mental picture of all the encouraging things I would say to the adult students who had come out of their long years of shame to finally learn how to read. I would talk about how they could read to their kids and finally help them with their homework; how they could read the labels on the items in the grocery store; and how they no longer had to be ashamed because they needed someone else to read their mail. I planned to explain how reading was a critical life skill that would open doors and change their lives forever. However, there was only one problem—the students were not my audience. Speaking to a group of professionals who are volunteers who want to help improve adult literacy completely changed the dynamics of my presentation. My theme changed from self-determination to communal responsibility.

Adopting the principle of *audience-focused preparation* will alleviate the critical error of what I call **"right message, wrong audience."**

Let's explore the principle of *audience-focused preparation* in more detail by reviewing two foundational justifications.

AUDIENCE-FOCUSED PREPARATION

Justification #1—The Psychology of Self-Interest

The psychology of self-interest is based on the premise that self-preservation and self-advancement are the two dominate principles that govern most human interaction. Arthur Schopenhauer wrote, "Most men are so thoroughly subjective that nothing really interests them but themselves." From our desire to preserve and advance self, we filter information through a prism of SELF-INTEREST. Many psychoanalyst have used the motive of self-interest as a basis for understanding what drives human behavior both individually and collectively. You don't have to read psychological journals to understand this concept; we practice it on a daily basis. Do you remember when you were a student and you took individual and group pictures with your class? When you reviewed the group photo who did you look for first? I can hear you say "ME"! You were deeply concerned about how you (self) looked before you even thought about anyone else in the photo. Why? Maybe you wanted to make sure that pimple on your nose didn't show up in the picture. Maybe you were concerned about your weight. Maybe you wanted to make sure your hair was perfect because you liked a boy in your class. Maybe you wanted to see if the designer symbol on your shirt was visible. Whatever the reason, it was motivated by self-interest. This principle also dominates our international relations and foreign policy decisions as a nation. Inherent in every foreign policy decision is the question: how will this policy preserve our way of life and advance our interest as a nation?

How does this principle apply to audience-focused preparation? **Your audience wants to know—what's in it for me?**

Why should I give you my attention and valuable time? How will your presentation benefit me?

For example, if you are a political consultant speaking to the national leadership of a particular political party, giving statistics and demographic information about voters is irrelevant if you don't demonstrate how said information will help their candidate(s) win the next election. It is imperative that you understand and master this principle.

Audience-focused preparation requires the consultant to prepare a presentation that will answer the most pressing question of the target audience: how will your presentation help me help my party win? Understanding the psychology of self-interest will help you organize, interpret, and present your information in such a way that will captivate the attention of your audience. Think back to when you heard a speaker that captivated your attention. What was it about the presentation that captured and kept your attention? I'm sure it had something to do with how it related in some way to your self-Interest. *Audience-focused preparation* is the North Star that should guide your research so that you will prepare the right message for the right audience.

Justification #2 — Relevancy in Context

Not only must your presentation appeal to the self-interest of your audience but your presentation must also be relevant within the context of the occasion. Your message to a graduating class of high school students will not be the same for the graduating class of a leadership institute of experienced business executives. Once you have received your invitation to speak, you must ask specific questions to ascertain exactly to whom you will be speaking, the context of the occasion, and the audience's expectations.

For example, if you are conducting a workshop on leadership for a group of business executives being out performed by their competitors due to innovation and leadership, you should customize your presentation to demonstrate how leadership affects quality, innovation, and the company's bottom line and position in the marketplace. You must be willing to adjust canned presentations so that they are relevant to the audience's self-interest. In order to do this, you must obtain relevant preliminary information through the audience analysis process (speaker's request form).

Principles for Audience Analysis

Below are five principles to help you develop the proper questions for your speaker's request form:

1. Make sure you find out the five Ws for the event: who, what, when, where and why. Note: This information should be on the written invitation from the event organizers.

2. Make sure you understand the history of the host organization and the significance of the occasion to the audience.

3. Make sure you get specific demographic information.

4. Make sure you understand the beliefs, values, and interest of your audience.

5. Make sure you ascertain the audience's expectations of you as a speaker. See the sample speaker's request form (survey) designed to acquire all of the information a speaker will need to prepare an audience-focused presentation.

Sample Speaker's Request Form (Survey)

1. What is the purpose of this event?

2. What are the three main takeaways you would like your audience to receive from the speaker's presentation?

3. What activities take place immediately before and after the program? (Please send program outline if possible.)

4. What are some current problems/opportunities, break-throughs occurring in your organization? (Please send history of your organization if not on your website.)

5. What are the most important challenges faced by the people who will be in the audience?

6. Will the audience be a group of experts in a particular field? If so, explain.

7. Does the audience have a particular political affiliation?

8. Does the audience have a particular religious affiliation?

9. How many attendees do you expect?

10. What is the ethnic makeup of the audience?

11. What is the age range of the audience?

12. What is the male/female ratio of attendees?

Obtaining answers to these questions will help you prepare a more customized presentation with information that is relevant to your target audience. Learning that your audience is gender-specific will help you tailor your presentation to better relate to that specific gender. For example, sports analogies may not be the best choice when trying to explain something to a group of women ages 40 to 65. I'm not implying that women don't know sports. My point is this: using sports examples would probably be a poor choice for this target audience. On the other hand, using sports analogies while speaking to a group of men between the ages of 24 and 35, would be more relevant to the target audience's frame of reference.

Marketing executives understand and practice this critical concept when devising marketing campaigns to sell their client's products/services. Once a specific target market is identified, then an audience appropriate message is developed to reach that target market. The market (audience) research precedes the message. Utilizing the audience-focused principle as a framework for research is the marketing/advertising industry's key to success. Now that we live in a more connected world through social media platforms, you must ask yourselves the following questions:

1. What is the benefit to social media companies to have my "profile information" in their databases?

2. Why do advertisers pay social media companies billions of dollars to reach specific consumers that fit a predetermined "profile" of their prospective customers?

Commercial marketers know that their costly digital, broadcast, and print messages will be ignored if not distributed to the right audience.

The three benefits of the audience analysis process (speaker's request form) are threefold:

1. You will obtain critical demographic information— age, gender, religion, racial, ethnic, and group affiliation.

2. You will obtain information about the beliefs, values, and attitudes of the audience prior to the occasion.

3. From your preliminary data, you will be able to ascertain the organizer's expectations of you as a speaker within the context of the occasion before the speech-writing process.

To sum it up, what are the best practices for audience analysis?

1. **Formalize the information-gathering process.** Once you receive an invitation to speak, you should send the organizer a detailed audience analysis survey (speaker's request form) that will ask the right questions to help you develop an accurate audience profile.

2. **Understand the context of the occasion.** For example, if you are speaking at a memorial service, you must be cognizant of the mood of the audience. Your presentation should honor the person being memorialized while inspiring and giving hope to the bereaved. Great speakers understand and know that the context of an occasion sets parameters that keep their remarks focused. A focused presentation must have parameters to keep the presenter focused on communicating an appropriate presentation within the context of the occasion. Telling distasteful jokes or voicing your conflicting political policy positions at a memorial service is highly inappropriate for the occasion.

As I am writing, I am watching the memorial service for the late Senator Edward Kennedy. This would be the wrong time for any speaker, especially the President of United States, to express his policy position on the pending health care reform bill. No matter how right you may think your message is, it would be inappropriate for the mood and context of the occasion, even though several policymakers who will vote on the bill are present. The Senate floor, a town hall meeting, and a political convention are the appropriate venues and occasions for such discourse.

3. **Understand the beliefs and values of your audience.** Understanding the values and beliefs of your audience will help you to understand what really drives their self-interest. Oftentimes we share the same beliefs and values of people from different political parties and religions but are not consciously aware of it.

Although I vehemently disagreed with many of the late President Ronald Reagan's economic policies, one of the reasons he was considered to be such a great communicator was not only due to his oratorical ability but also due to his ability to cloak controversial and complex policy positions in universal values and principles that most Americans shared. In his book *Eyewitness to Power*, former Reagan speechwriter David Gergen points out, "Liberty, heroism, honor, a love of country, a love of God. Those were notions that sophisticates tend to dismiss as platitudes, or worse. However, they went deep with Reagan, and as he had discovered from years on the speaking circuit, they went deep with most Americans." Because the majority of Americans love God and their country, Reagan understood how to connect, even with those who vehemently opposed him politically. The themes of life, liberty, heroism, honor, and love of country were often cloaked in stories Reagan told.

The power of storytelling and the narrative method of speech writing was Reagan's way of connecting with millions of American people via mass media. Consider the following excerpt from a 1984 speech Ronald Reagan gave entitled, "Our Noble Vision: An Opportunity for All":

> Not long ago I received a letter from a young woman named Kim. She was born with the birth defect spina bifida and given little chance to live. But her parents were willing to try a difficult and risky operation on her spine. It worked. And Kim wrote me: "I am now 24 years old. I do have some medical problems due to my birth defect. I have a lot of problems with my legs. But I'm walking. I can talk. I went to grade and high school, plus one year of college. I thank God every day for my parents and my life." And Kim said, "I wouldn't change it if I could." Life was her greatest opportunity, and she's made the most of it.

Reagan used this story to drive home the point that every child should have the right to life no matter what the circumstances. This was his way of connecting the life of a real person to his pro-life position. David Gergen continues, "Reagan's stories made his intangible principles come to life and linked ordinary Americans to the values he so often espoused. They were a critical part of his connection with his followers. The two went together: the values informed the stories and the stories brought the values to life."

Moreover, telling your own personal story can be the most powerful way to connect your values and beliefs with those of your audience. You may be virtually unknown to your audience, so they want to know: who are you? They want to know if they can identify with you in some way. They want to know if you have similar struggles and obstacles, and how you overcame them. They want to know if they can learn something from your experience(s) that will help them get through their current situation or predicament. Being transparent with your audience and revealing something about yourself is a very effective method to personalize universal values and beliefs.

This reminds me of a situation when I was a member of the TSU Debate Team. We were in competition in Ohio, and I participated in an individual event called "original prose." This event required participants to tell an original story authored by the participant. I vividly remember sitting in the university library prior to boarding the van and collecting my thoughts about what to write. I decided to tell my personal story of the passing of my father and its impact on me as a thirteen-year old child. Most participants wrote out stories and memorized them word-for-word, which took away some of its authenticity. I didn't have to do that; I could tell my story straight from the heart. At the time, I must admit, I really didn't understand the power of **audience-connection through personal transparency.** To be honest with you, I was just trying to get through the round so that I could focus on the events that were considered my stronger events because I had memorized all the information word-for-word. To my surprise, I made it to finals and was floored when I won first place at the awards ceremony.

People feel more comfortable with someone they can identify with—laugh with, cry with, and go on a journey of discovery with. If possible, get to know your audience by understanding their values and beliefs in advance. This principle is especially true when speaking to highly sensitive *belief-centered audiences* like Christians, Jews,

Muslims, Democrats, Republicans, etc. For example, you don't have to be a Christian to point out how compassionate Jesus was to his followers and enemies as recorded in the gospels. This can be used to teach the theme of compassion from the belief-centered audience's perspective. Believe it or not, there are more universal themes and principles in the three major religions of Christianity, Judaism, and Islam than we realize. My point is this: even if you are speaking to an audience with a different religious persuasion from your own, you can still find some universal principles from your religion that are applicable to their beliefs.

THE "WE" PRINCIPLE

The "we" principle is a strategy many high profile speakers use to stir collective inspiration and action from an audience. The "Yes We Can!" slogan coined by President Barack Obama's presidential campaign embodied this principle. When you say "we," you figuratively put yourself in the same boat with your audience. We will rise or sink together!

Dr. King put it best when he said, "We are all tied together in a single garment of destiny." People are more likely to believe in what you have to say if they believe you are talking to them and not at or down to them. When I speak to at-risk youth in urban communities, I often tell my personal story of how my poor decision-making as a teen almost got my mother killed. While telling my story, I always notice how eyebrows begin to rise and heads lean forward when I tell them I was extremely at-risk, considering some of the counterproductive behavior I engaged in as a teen. One of the comments I received on my evaluation form from one student summed it up, "If you can be successful, I can be successful!"

—————— SECTION III ——————
Always Start with Purpose

PRINCIPLE
Always Start With Your End Result First

After you understand who your audience is and the context of the event, you can start the process of selecting a topic for your speech. Topic selection and the content of your speech will come from the stated purpose of your presentation. The principle of purpose dictates that you know the end-result of something before you begin. For example, Johnnie Cochran knew that the purpose for his trial presentation in the O.J. Simpson trial was to raise reasonable doubt, not to prove O.J.'s innocence. Raising "reasonable doubt" was the organizing principle and purpose for all of his research, as well as his written and oral arguments. Cochran's famous catchy slogan, "If it don't fit, you must acquit," was not an accident. It was coined within the context of purpose— proving that there was justifiable "reasonable doubt" about Simpson's guilt. Once you identify the desired end-result of your presentation, you are on your way to communicating the right message to the right audience.

MAP IT OUT: DEVELOP YOUR TRAVEL PLANS (OUTLINE)

Developing your outline is an effective preparation tool to help you communicate your stated purpose and organize the structure and flow of your presentation. When I enter an address in my global positioning system (GPS), it gives me a map with step-by-step directions of how to get to my destination. My GPS gets me there before I even leave the comfort of my home. That's what a good outline will do;

66

it will give you a road map to a great presentation before you leave home. Consider the outline below for one of my presentations.

SPEECH OUTLINE

Purpose: To communicate to teens ages 15-17 how their belief system determines who they will become.

Topic: "Get Your Mind Right"

Outline

   I. Explain the purpose of the belief system

      A. Decision-making

      B. Behavior and habits

  II. How can you as an individual purposefully influence your belief system?

      A. Knowledge acquisition

      B. Empowerment affirmations and actions

 III. Explain the belief system cycle

      A. Thoughts, decisions, actions, and habits reinforce each other, creating a cycle

      B. Your belief system is a reflection of who you are

 IV. Q & A

Outlining your speech gives you a clear and concise game plan for achieving your stated purpose. All speeches should start with purpose first, then topic and points/sub-points. This is why the speaker's request form is so important. You can't map out your destination until you know where you are going and why.

KNOW YOUR TERRAIN: GET INTELLIGENCE AND SCOUT OUT THE PROMISED LAND

As I mentioned earlier, you may want to go to the actual location where you will be speaking, not only to familiarize yourself with the facility, but also to be proactive and resolve potential problems before they happen.

Listed below is a list of things to look for when scouting out a location:

1. Quality of the sound system. **Note:** All sound system issues should be resolved prior to the event. If the sound system is horrible, call the organizers and request that an external sound system be provided for the presentation. Recently, I attended an event hosted by a university where Stedman Graham was the keynote speaker. The sound system was horrible and disrupted his presentation several times. The university organizer could have mitigated this issue prior to the event by testing the system in advance and making the necessary corrections. The speaker was visibly perturbed, and you could see it on his face.

2. Will there be a sound technician on site operating the system the day of the event?

3. If you will use visual aides such as a projector, screen, DVD player, etc., you must work out all technical difficulties prior to the presentation. Find out who the technical person will be, and do a dry run. **Note:** Sometimes technology can fail, so have a contingency plan in place to continue your presentation without your visual aids.

4. Will I have a microphone with a cord or a cordless mic? **Note:** Microphones with cords restrict your ability to walk around. You may even want to request a lapel microphone if you like to have your hands free.

5. Is there a podium?

6. Make sure that there will not be too many extra lights on you, which will cause sweating. **Note:** Sweating will make you look nervous and uneasy.

7. Make sure that extra lighting will not blind you from seeing your audience. It's hard to make an audience connection if you can't see them.

8. Observe the seating arrangement and ask the event coordinator if this is how the room will be set up during the actual event.

9. If you are speaking during a luncheon or dinner, ask the organizers to notify the servers to minimize the noise during the presentation. The clicking and clacking in the kitchen will be a distraction while you are speaking.

In the final analysis, preparation requires discipline. Discipline is the key to mastering the law of preparation. You must develop your plan of action and execute it according to time specific benchmarks. The discipline you exert in private will manifest itself in your stage presence, demeanor, and confidence. Doc's mastery of disciplined preparation is one of the reasons that he has such a commanding stage presence. His private discipline radiates through his body language, projecting his level of mastery. When you meet him, you know that you are in the presence of greatness.

LAW III
SPEAK BEFORE YOU SPEAK

LAW III

SPEAK BEFORE YOU SPEAK

LAW DEFINED

The conscious awareness that you have the power to influence your body language (nonverbal expressions) to communicate a message of your choice.

PRINCIPLE

Your Body Carries a "Message of Your Choice"

THE POWER OF NONVERBAL COMMUNICATION

According to body language expert Jeanine Driver, research has shown that just 7% of human communication is done through actual words.[1] This means that 93% of what we communicate is nonverbal. As a case study, body language experts are still studying the first televised Kennedy-Nixon debate. Most listeners who heard the debate on the radio thought that Nixon had won. However, viewers who watched the televised debate thought Senator Kennedy had won. Here are some of the paraphrased observations that body language experts have made:

Nixon
- Excessive sweating and using a handkerchief to constantly wipe his face.
- Pale, unfit, and sickly looking.

- Fidgeting.
- Excessive blinking and unfavorable facial expressions.
- Looked fatigued.
- Unsure of himself.
- Uncomfortable gestures that signaled anxiety.
- Attire (light gray baggy suit) that didn't look good on the new medium of communication (black and white TV).

Kennedy
- Poised and in command of his posture.
- Tanned, fit, and healthy looking.
- Looked well rested and refreshed.
- Appeared confident and sure of himself.
- Appropriate attire (dark custom-fit suit).

The nonverbal bottom line is this: Senator Kennedy LOOKED more presidential than Vice President Nixon.

Listed below are five critical nonverbal communication characteristics you should strive to improve.

1. **The Way You Walk**

   Advice: Always walk with your head up, shoulders and back straight to project an image of confidence. The same rule applies when standing to address your audience.

2. **Handshake**

   Advice: Always give firm handshakes.

3. **Eye Contact**

    Advice: In most cases, make eye contact, especially when shaking hands. There are some cultures where eye contact is disrespectful. Learn who your audience is and what their customs are during the preparation stage.

4. **Facial Expressions**

    Advice: Never make expressions of dislike or boredom when interacting with an audience. Do your best to smile and make pleasant facial expressions.

5. **Body Movements**

    Advice: Your body movements should be calm and poised, which is an illustration of your confidence, presence, and self-mastery. Don't fidget and play with your hands or look nervous!

I could sense and feel Doc's self-mastery, presence, and confidence just by watching him walk into a room. Although he is relatively a small man in physical size (maybe 5'9" in height and 130 pounds), he seems to command his personal space with the authority of an 8 foot, 400 pound giant.

What is your body saying? Long before you open your mouth to say anything, your body is communicating with your audience. If a speaker walks into a room with his head down, appearing to be nervous, timid, and lacking self-confidence, the audience has already begun to pass unfavorable judgments about his credibility. He's scared; he's unprepared; I don't want to hear anything this guy has to say because he's certainly no expert. Well, you may ask yourself, how did certain members of the audience come to such conclusions without the speaker even speaking?

73

That's my point: you speak before you speak. Your body language is sending out messages whether you like it or not. You must be cognizant of your ability to influence your nonverbal expressions with a "message of your choice." For example, if you are nervous, don't let everyone know it by visibly showing it on your face. You should look confident by:

1. Believing that all your **"disciplined preparation"** will pay off.

2. Feeling confident because you "know you have a voice" and you have something of "value" to say.

3. Making eye contact with your audience.

4. Expressing interest in speakers on the program before you.

5. Making facial expressions that convey seriousness of purpose.

Nonverbal expression is a powerful method of communication, and most people are not cognizant of its ability to make or break their presentation.

YOUR BODY CAN TALK!

It is estimated that more than 700,000 physical signals can be sent through bodily movement.[2]

Kinesics is the study and interpretation of body language— gestures, facial expressions, and body motions. We communicate nonverbally every day when communicating with friends, family, and coworkers. Think about the confused look on your face when your friend told you she was going back to the same guy that she said was a jerk last week. Before you could say anything, your facial expressions spoke for you, eliciting a response of "Don't look at me like that!" Your friend more than likely interpreted your unpleasant facial expressions as one of disapproval and judgment.

Perhaps you recall a time when you were disciplining one of your children, and you became even more upset due to the child's indifferent body language. This may have made you feel that the child didn't care or was not listening to you. Another example would be the confused look on a student's face which is a nonverbal signal to the teacher to explain the information in more detail. We all interpret body language on a daily basis and must understand how our potential audience will interpret what our body has to say.

From the moment you walk into a room and begin interacting with the audience, your handshake, eye contact, gestures, and body movements are sending very important messages about you to your audience. A firm handshake coupled with great eye contact will most likely be interpreted as confidence. In contrast, barely shaking hands and avoiding eye contact could be interpreted as timidity, nervousness, or perhaps; arrogance. Remember, people are not just listening to hear what you have to say, they are also watching and will instinctively interpret what your body has to say, which leads me to the principle of **synchronized communication.**

Synchronized communication simply means your nonverbal expressions complement and enhance your verbal message. When this happens, you are operating in the **"one body, one message"** domain of public speaking.

Let's explore this concept in more detail.

One Body, One Message

After hearing and watching Dr. Freeman speak on several occasions, I clearly understand the power of the "**one body, one message**" concept. For example, Doc's voice inflections, speech content, and body language complemented each other, creating a "spirit of unity," which maximized the full impact of his message. If he were making a point that required expressing joy, he would project the most infectious smile I have ever seen. If he were making a point that required expressing seriousness of thought, he would project the demeanor of a scholar in deep thought. If he were making a point using a high-pitched tone of voice, his hands would go up in an upward motion to put extra emphasis on that point. Dr. Freeman's body language always captured the appropriate emotion he intended to communicate to the audience. An effective communicator must know how to stir up the emotions of an audience by becoming a temporary embodiment of the emotion itself. This requires **synchronized communication** of both verbal and nonverbal expression, which brings harmony to your message.

Former President Clinton is a master of this technique. He knows how to communicate sincerity by using the right words, tone of voice, eye contact, facial expressions, and head movements. Most importantly, he knows how to be, in the moment, the emotion he intends to communicate. As a presidential candidate, this was one of the factors that propelled him to the presidency—**believability.** How else could an unknown governor from Arkansas become president of the most powerful nation on earth unless the electorate believed in him?

Great communicators must be believable, and that is the ultimate purpose of the **"one body, one message"** concept. In order for this to happen, there is no room for a contradiction between your words and your body language. Both must be on the same page and communicating the same message. This is why some trial attorneys hire body language experts to assess not only what a witness is saying, but also the truth of their nonverbal expressions. A witness with contradictory verbal and nonverbal messages is a red flag that alerts the jury that something is not quite right. You don't have to be a body-language expert to ascertain the authenticity or believability of a speaker. This is why the first lesson in this book clearly explains the concept of mastering your mental self. It is from this mastery that your nonverbal communication will be in total harmony with your body's total self-expression. The appropriate nonverbal expressions should come naturally and not be forced. Don't divide your attention by trying to monitor your body language during the presentation. Recent brain research shows that natural, unstudied gestures express emotions or impulses a split second before our thought processes have turned them into words.[3] Trying to calculate when to use the appropriate gesture is a recipe for disaster. However, in order to perfect your presentation, you need to correct gestures that serve as distractions. How do you do this? You need to see yourself in action.

LAW IN PRACTICE

Practice your presentation in front of the mirror or with a video recorder and carefully observe your posture, facial expressions, and gestures. This exercise will allow you to see what others are seeing. Think of it this way: if you were watching yourself, what would be your honest evaluation of yourself? What are your nonverbal expressions communicating? When I was a member of the debate team, in order to improve my effectiveness, I recorded myself and practiced in front of the mirror several weeks before a competition. As a result, I witnessed a dramatic increase in my speaking skills and awards. I am not giving you theory from some book; this tactic actually worked for me with great success. Constructive self-observation will allow you to assess weak areas, make adjustments, and improve the overall quality of your presentation. This exercise will also help you improve your stage presence and your overall appearance.

Mastering the **"one body, one message"** principle is a critical milestone to becoming a great communicator. As a communicator, it is your responsibility to ensure that your body, soul, and spirit all say the same thing. This is why body-language experts, as well as average untrained people, can detect when you're not being honest. **Your body language will tell the truth on you!**

A FRAMEWORK FOR READING BODY LANGUAGE

One common misperception about reading body language is that all gestures, expressions, and body movement mean the same thing. According to body language expert Dr. Ann Beall, "Using a framework is the most useful way to decode others, because a combination of behaviors tells a story."[4] Below is Dr. Ann Beall's framework for decoding body language: PERCEIVE.

PERCEIVE stands for:

- Proximity
- Expressions
- Relative Orientation
- Contact
- Eyes
- Individual Gestures
- Voice
- Existence of Adapters

Proximity is the distance between individuals. Generally, people sit, stand, and want to be near those they like. Increased proximity is an indication of feelings of liking and interest.

Expressions are observed on the face and can last as little as 1/15 of a second. These very brief expressions are called micro-expressions, and they occur when people are trying to hide a feeling. Interestingly, when people begin to experience an emotion, their facial muscles are triggered. If they suppress the expression, it's shown for only 1/15 of a second. If they do not suppress it, the expression will appear prominently. The six universal expressions that all cultures recognize are **happiness, sadness, anger, fear, surprise, and disgust.**

Relative orientation is the degree to which people face one another. A parallel orientation indicates that one is interested in and focused on the other person. As people become less interested in and less focused on another person, they tend to angle their bodies away. A good way to

79

decode orientation is to observe where a person's feet are placed. Often people will point their feet in the direction they truly want to go.

Contact refers to physical contact. Generally, the amount and frequency of physical contact demonstrates closeness, familiarity, and degree of liking. A lot of touching indicates strong liking for another person.

Eyes primarily show whom or what people are most interested in or like. One can gauge liking and interest by the frequency, duration, and total amount of time spent looking.

Individual gestures can indicate an image in a person's mind that is sometimes not communicated with spoken **language.** Some typical gestures are ones in which people indicate what refers to them and what refers to others (e.g., the hands come near the **body** or motion away), gestures that describe an emotion or experience (e.g., sobbing gesture or frenetic moving of the hands), or gestures that identify where objects are in relation to one another. Gestures can provide information about how things are organized in a person's mind. They can also reveal how people are feeling; people tend to gesture more when they are enthusiastic, excited, and energized. People gesture less when they are demoralized, nervous, or concerned about the impression they are making.

Voice, or speech, provides much information about the demographics of a speaker (e.g., gender, age, area of origin, social class). Voice can also reveal emotions, which are transmitted through the tone of the voice, accentuation of words, rapidity of speech, and number of speech errors.

Typically, speech errors indicate discomfort and anxiety, a person who begins to make many speech errors may be anxious and ill at ease.

Existence of adapters is the last piece of PERCEIVE. Adapters are small behaviors that tend to occur when people are stressed or bored with a situation. Examples are playing with rings, twirling a pen, or touching one's hair. As meetings extend, an increasing number of adapter behaviors tend to emerge among the people in the room.

My purpose in giving you this framework is to help you start the process of learning a new language called "body language." Armed with this new language, you will be able to decipher what others are really saying, especially yourself.

Before I advance to the next law, it is extremely imperative that I point out the importance of physical appearance, which consists of attire and grooming.

ATTIRE

The way you dress also sends subtle messages to your audience. For both men and women, executive business attire should be worn to most speaking engagements. There are always exceptions, (i.e. speaking at a kick-off rally for a walkathon). Use your common sense and good judgment on this one. If you are not sure, ask the organizers who invited you what the appropriate attire is for this occasion. Your attire helps to build or tear down your credibility. People might have a hard time believing you are an expert in mergers and acquisitions if you have on a t-shirt and sweatpants, especially if you are unknown.

GROOMING

Both men and women should always present a crisp, clean appearance. Numerous studies have confirmed that a speaker's personal appearance plays a major role in his or her acceptance as a credible speaker.[5] Men should always be shaven with a nice, clean haircut. Women should have their hair styled to their liking to complement their well-coordinated attire.

The bottom line is this: well-coordinated attire and grooming produces a pristine appearance, which communicates the message to your audience—"You can trust me and my message."

One Body, One Message

LAW IV
SPEAK WHEN YOU SPEAK

Law IV

Speak When You Speak

Law Defined

The art of knowing how to skillfully deliver the right message to the right audience at the right time.

Principle
Get the Attention of Your Audience, and Keep It!

After hours of disciplined preparation, now it's time to finally speak.

Law IV, **"speak when you speak"** means exactly what it says. When you stand before an audience, you need to not only have great content, but also a great delivery. How you say what you have to say is just as important as what you have to say. You must deliver the right message to the right audience at the right time. A great speech on paper means nothing if 1) The speaker doesn't know how to bring the text to life with the power of the spoken word, and 2) the speaker delivers a great message to the wrong audience. As a disclaimer, I must emphasize that there is no substitute for great content. If your content is poor, then your great delivery will be null and void. You must develop your content in the preparation phase to set the stage for a great delivery. The first rule of giving an excellent delivery is to get the attention of your audience. How are you going to let them know that you have something of value to say? How

85

are you going to establish rapport and make a connection with your audience? How are you going to deal with the competing interest for your audience's attention? Listed below are specific attention-getting methods that you can use to capture the attention of your audience.

Ways to Capture Audience Attention

Peak Curiosity

I vividly remember how Doc began one of his speeches while addressing the annual convocation for incoming freshmen. Doc boldly walked to the podium and began his presentation in an elevated tone of voice:

"Thank you for that gracious introduction. Upon receiving the invitation to deliver the opening convocation address, I concluded that I should aim to put into effect the three S's of successful public speaking. The first, stand up to be seen, and that I just did! The second, speak up to be heard, and that I am doing now! The third, shut up to be appreciated, and that I shall do, after I have addressed you within the time constraint, on the subject: No Time for Tears...No Time for Tears."

Although Doc's speech was not about public speaking, he used the topic to get the attention of his audience. Doc knows that the fear of public speaking is a misplaced insecurity that affects many freshmen. His strategy was to get the attention of his audience by giving them the principles of how to be a successful public speaker; then, he demonstrated the principles in his presentation with his selected topic: "No Time for Tears." When he gave his opening statement in his deep baritone celestial voice, **"The three S's of successful public speaking!"** I saw heads turn and eyebrows go up because Doc's voice has a way of touching something deep within your core.

Doc's unique speaking style coupled with the information of how to be a successful public speaker definitely captured the attention of the audience and peaked their curiosity. You must generate interest from your audience by using your unique speaking style to skillfully communicate information that stirs the imagination. **Remember**: *No matter how good the content of your speech may be, you must project and inflect your voice to avoid sounding monotone and boring.* The last thing people want to hear is a speaker that will bore them to sleep. The opportunity to get the attention of your audience must be seized with all available force, tact, and creativity in the beginning of your presentation. You only have one time to make a first impression—don't mess it up.

The Shock-Value Tactic

The shock-value tactic allows you to use extreme information to point out the seriousness of a particular issue that is relevant to the audience. For example, quoting statistics with a "shock value" is an effective way to get the attention of your audience.

Consider this startling statistic: "In 2004, firearm homicide was the number one cause of death for 15-34 year-old African Americans." This statistic would definitely get the attention of an African American audience with its inherent shock value. The shock-value tactic is an excellent way to get the attention of an audience who is mostly affected by the "shocking" information. This method can also be cross-applied to other tactics mentioned in this section. Statistics and personal stories work best with this approach.

Rhetorical Questions

A rhetorical question is a question that is asked by the speaker but not actually answered by the audience. The purpose of this tactic is to focus the attention of your audience on the central theme of your message. Asking a rhetorical question of your audience is a way not only to get the attention of your audience, but also a way to let your audience know that your speech will be relevant and beneficial to them in some way. For instance, if you ask the question: How would you like to fire your boss, start your own business, and control your own destiny? You have immediately established the basis and purpose of your speech while appealing to the self-interest of your audience. Now they are listening because they want to know how you can help them get out of the rat race.

Storytelling

Personal Stories

As I mentioned earlier, storytelling is an effective way to make a connection with your audience. This tactic can serve dual purposes if you decide to open your speech with a relevant story. Notice I said relevant. Your story must, in some way, be relevant to the major themes in your speech and the overall message. I vividly remember the attention-getting story Doc told as he began his eulogy of the late Barbara Jordan. "When I last saw Barbara it was at a Martin Luther King concert by the Chicago Sinfonietta conducted by Paul Freeman, where Barbara said, as the narrator following the introduction, 'I am pleased to be here not only with Tom's (Doc's) brother Paul but just to hear Tom introduce me. In fact, I always like to hear him introduce me because he always makes me feel as though I am somebody.' It was not necessary to make Barbara feel like somebody—she was somebody!"

I will never forget the awe-stricken look on then President Bill Clinton's face as Doc went on to mesmerize the audience with his animated body movements and the colorful language he used to paint a poetic picture of Barbara as he knew her. Although this was a state funeral service with a somber atmosphere, the audience gave Doc a standing ovation. If you want to see Doc's remarks for yourself, go to *http://www.c-spanvideo.org/program/69467-1* or simply Google "Barbara Jordan's Funeral Service." At the end of this chapter, you may read this speech in its entirety with comments embedded in the text to point out best practices for an effective delivery.

Fictional Stories

As I reflect on the treasured memories I have of Doc's speeches, I recall a modified story he would tell about the man, the boy, and the donkey. The paraphrased version of the story goes like this:

> A young boy and his father started out on a journey walking to town with their donkey. As they walked, a countryman passed them and said, "You fools, what is a donkey for but to ride?" So, the father put the boy on the donkey and they continued to town. Soon they passed a group of men, one of whom said, "See that lazy youngster; he lets his father walk while he rides." Therefore, the father ordered his boy to get off, and he got on. They soon passed several women who said, "Shame on that lazy man to let his poor little son trudge along." So, the father decided to allow both of them to ride the donkey.

The story ends with all of them falling off the bridge and drowning. This story was used to drive home the themes of personal responsibility and decision-making. Doc concluded the story by boldly saying, "You can't please everybody!"

Utilizing the story got the attention of the audience because it took you on a journey. Great stories always take you on a journey that, in the end, provides visual lessons for the audience. Consider the story below and the lessons I extract from the story to make relevant points in a speech I delivered to a community-based organization.

> The story begins in an English colony with a middle-aged man named Rip Van Winkle. Rip was an average guy who was kind of a slacker who avoided work and didn't always do what was in his best interest.
>
> One day Rip went deep into the mountains to get away from his troubles. While there, Rip decided to take what he thought would be a short nap. When Rip awoke, he discovered he had aged, and things just didn't seem the same. When he made his way back to town, he noticed the different clothing the people wore; he noticed the new buildings and nicely paved streets; he noticed that he didn't recognize any of the townspeople; and he noticed that the picture of the King that was once placed so prominently in the town square had been replaced by some guy called President George Washington. When Rip asked one of the townsmen who this man was and where is the picture of our beloved King, the man explained to him that the American Revolution had taken place and now the colony was New York, a state of the newly formed United States of America.
>
> To Rip's dismay; he discovered that he had been asleep for 20 years.
>
> What's the lesson here?
>
> Don't get caught sleeping during times of great social, political, and economic change. When individuals, communities, and organizations are asleep during times of great change, we become insignificant and have no seat at the table.
>
> Now is the time to wake up, take our communities

back, and lead the next wave of change in Houston, Texas.

Now is no time to sleep because our children are still dropping out of school and dropping into jails!

I have used this tactic with much success. Utilizing relevant fictional stories in your speech will help you put your themes and key points into perspective for the audience.

Quotes

Starting with a quote can be a powerful way to put your presentation into perspective. Consider this quote by Malcolm X: "Education is our passport to the future, for tomorrow belongs to the people who prepare for it today." This quote puts into perspective the purpose of education and why we must pursue it. If I were talking to a group of high school students about staying in school, this would be the perfect quote to get their attention.

Consider the quotes below:

Change is the law of life. And those who look only to the past or present are certain to miss the future.
President John F. Kennedy

Note: This quote can be used to support the theme of change.

What the people want is very simple. They want an America as good as its promise.
Congresswoman Barbara Jordan

Note: This quote can be used to promote a message of institutional accountability.

I submit to you that if a man hasn't discovered something he will die for, he isn't fit to live.
Dr. Martin Luther King, Jr.

Note: This quote can be used to support the theme of commitment.

Themes are often broad and abstract, but the right quote will bring them to life. There are several other audience **attention-getting** tactics you can further research—humor, audio/visual aids, something relevant and unique to the occasion, etc.

Delivery

Now that you have the attention of your audience, you must keep it!

Getting the attention of your audience is a great first step, but now you must present your information and convey your themes in a way that will consume your audience's attention and focus. Your objective is to get your audience completely immersed in your presentation and clinging to your every word by using the following delivery tactics.

1. **Master Diction and Voice Quality.**

    Diction is choice of words, especially with regard to correctness, clearness, or effectiveness.[1] Most of Doc's students, and those who have heard him speak, will agree with me that his unique voice quality and razor sharp enunciation are definitely factors that have contributed to his ability to keep an audience dazzled and engaged throughout his entire presentation. I'm not suggesting that you should speak like Doc; he has his own unique style and so should you. My intention is not to encourage emulation but to point out techniques that you should use within the context of your own speaking style. Remember, my goal is to help you find your voice. I'm reminded of an incident that gives me great perspective on not trying to emulate someone else. When I first met Doc in his office, I was so impressed with the way he recited a prose piece that I tried to emulate his every movement and voice modulation while reciting the same piece in competition. I received feedback from one judge telling me, "There will never be another Dr. Freeman. Be yourself."

Being original and authentic is the foundation for your success as a public speaker. As I reflect on Doc's superior and well-developed diction, it seemed like he surgically enunciated every syllable of every word to give it maximum verbal impact. He didn't stumble over words; you clearly understood every word as he clearly articulated his ideas. You must develop the ability to stress important words and subordinate the less important words with the tone, pitch, and enunciation of your words. In the examples below, the bold-lettered words should be articulated with emphasis and meaning.

Example 1
*"**All** that **I** am, or **hope** to be, **I** owe to my **angel mother**."* Abraham Lincoln

Example 2
*"I learned that **courage** was not the **absence** of fear, but the **triumph** over it. The **brave man** is not he who does not **feel** afraid, but **he** who **conquers** that fear."*
Nelson Mandela

2. **Utilize Voice Inflection for Emphasis.**

Voice inflection is the art of projecting and changing the pitch, tone, and volume of your voice. Properly utilizing voice inflection empowers you to put emphasis on important points, signal transition from theme to theme, and avoid sounding monotone and downright boring. I can remember a few of my college professors who often gave lectures with great information, but their monotone delivery would put even the most caffeine-filled college student to sleep. Why have great content, but poor delivery? It's like putting a five-course lobster dinner on a trash can lid and saying, "Eat up!" This is why restaurants spend a significant amount of time and attention on details and delivery display in order to ensure that their meals are presented with just as much flavor as the meal itself.

President Barack Obama has mastered this critical public-speaking skill. If you study most of his campaign speeches, you will discover his mastery of **voice modulation and inflection** to emphasize certain points. The inflection

95

of his voice is what gives his speeches a lofty resounding effect that seems to carry you away. Doc has the same ability to use his words to carry his audience with him to the heights of the highest mountain. I know that you are thinking, "I don't need to sound lofty and preacher like for my board or classroom presentation. I just need to be effective." You can use this method on a less dramatic scale by using proper intonation.

For example, modulating the tone and pitch of your voice to emphasize a key point or indicate a transition from one point to the next is an excellent way to avoid the trap of sounding monotone. Most preachers use what I call the crescendo method, which involves starting out with a soft-spoken tone and pitch and gradually progressing to an elevated tone with great enthusiasm and energy. This extreme method may not be appropriate for a business presentation, so as a rule of thumb, just make sure your voice variations are used skillfully to highlight and emphasize major points.

There is no cookie cutter approach. You will develop your own unique style. Don't try to emulate or be someone else! Just be yourself, and if you are authentic, maybe someone will try to emulate you one day.

3. **Speaking with Passion.**

Nothing can compensate for passion. Utilizing

proper diction and inflection means nothing if you don't have passion. Passion is the spirit of your presentation. Just as the body cannot survive without a spirit, your speech will be dead without passion. When Doc speaks, his passion is often expressed in such a way that you literally connect with him and the poetic words being uttered. The aforementioned speech entitled, "No Time for Tears" was one of the most spirit-filled public addresses I have ever seen, heard, and felt. This speech was delivered to TSU's 1998 incoming freshman class, faculty, and staff. Doc took us on a mountain-top journey as he passionately expressed themes of perseverance, leadership, commitment, decision-making, personal responsibility, and love. That day, his passion was providential to say the least, and it is my belief that the spirit and passion of the speech came from his deeply anchored love for TSU. I advise my students and clients to always, if possible, select a topic that they are passionate about.

Remember: *Passion is the breath of life that will bring your presentation to life.*

MOST COMMON TYPES OF SPEECHES

There are many different types of speeches for different occasions: christenings, weddings, funerals, graduations, award ceremonies, inaugurals, retirement dinners, etc.[2] In this section, we will focus on three categories of speeches—motivational, informative, and persuasive.

Motivational

Motivational speeches are designed to inspire, inform, and persuade an audience. Below is a speech I wrote for a charter school speaking engagement for a client. I have changed the name of the school and altered some of the content to protect the client's identity.

Innovation Science Academy

Are you ready to innovate, compete, and lead in the new global economy?

Thursday, January 27

First and foremost, let me thank Principal Calvin Johnson and his very capable staff for the invitation to share in your educational experience this morning.

I feel honored to be in the presence of such intelligent young men and women who will be our future leaders. It is my expectation that every student in this room will play a major role in shaping the new global economy of the future.

So today, I simply want to ask the question: Are you ready to innovate, compete, and lead in the new global economy?

We truly live in a world where people and markets are connected like never before. Through our technological ingenuity and innovation we have made tremendous progress in making the world community a local community.

Because of our innovation and ingenuity, you can now be on a remote beach in Galveston, Texas, "chitchatting" on your lap top via social media with your friend in Johannesburg, South Africa.

Because of our innovation and ingenuity, students can now collaborate with their peers from around the world on various school projects, truly making their educational experience global.

Because of our innovation and ingenuity, scientists have discovered new worlds in DNA through the Human Genome project.

Because of our innovation and ingenuity, commerce moves at the speed of light, bringing buyers and sellers together in major markets around the world.

Because of our innovation, ingenuity, and the talent in this room, America has an opportunity to lead the global community in advances in transportation, science, technology, energy, medicine, education, and entrepreneurial ability if, and only if, we prepare future leaders like you with a relevant twenty-first century education.

My position on charter schools is this: if it works, let's duplicate it. We can't simply capitulate to special interest pressure at the expense of our children.

The best justification for the continued existence and expansion of charter schools is the excellence and success of our students. Innovation Science Academy has proven over and over again that "student excellence" can be achieved with the right leadership and educational model.

So today, I want to leave you with a few thoughts to ponder as you go back to class.

If you are going to be prepared to lead in the new global economy, you must have a strong background in math, science, and technology. Having a strong foundation in the "sciences" is a prerequisite for our future innovators, especially in the energy sector. One of the biggest challenges that our new leaders must confront is solving the problem of meeting our own, as well as the world's global, energy demands.

China is eating our lunch in this regard.

New York Times columnist Thomas Friedman consistently points out the long-term, multi-billion dollar investments that China is making in alternative energy innovation and manufacturing to eliminate the country's dependency on foreign energy. "Their investment in innovation to produce more electric cars powered by an alternative energy infrastructure— wind, solar, and biofuels—serves a dual purpose. Not only does it reduce their dependency on imported oil, but it creates jobs for its citizens. The auto industry was the foundation for America's manufacturing middle class. It allowed people with high school diplomas to earn a good living for their families. But those jobs are rapidly diminishing now."

So what does this mean to you?

It will take new innovators to retool the auto industry, which is a major employment sector in our country, and I believe it can start right here at Innovation Science Academy.

Friedman said in one of his editorials, "the country that replaces gasoline-powered vehicles with electric-powered vehicles — in an age of steadily rising oil prices and steadily falling battery prices — will have a huge cost advantage and independence from imported oil."

My point is this: the jobs and careers in the new global economy will be technical, knowledge-based, and heavily rooted in math, science, and technology. To all the students that were fortunate enough to be accepted to this school, you have what we call in the business world a "competitive advantage."

Your education and training must prepare you to compete in a global talent pool. As a former political staffer, it was my job to make sure my elected representative supported policies that helped Houston compete, not just with other cities in America, but with other cities in other countries.

Consider these facts: the Houston metropolitan area (MSA) is home to over 3,500 international companies, 23 fortune 500 companies, 21 foreign banks, over 900 freight forwarders, and 86 foreign consulates. All of our major employment centers like the Port of Houston, NASA, the Medical Center, and the Energy Corridor serve as a gateway to the international community. No one can deny the fact that Houston is truly a global city that is interconnected with people and markets on a global scale.

When you graduate from college, you must understand that you are competing with graduates from India as well as Indiana. You must take your education very seriously, or you will be left behind in an unforgiving global market that has no mercy for slackers. You are here to learn. Innovation Science Academy is your passport to a bright and prosperous future.

As our new political, business, and social leaders, it will be your responsibility to make sure your city remains a competitive city. When you graduate from college, stay in Houston and make a commitment to use your time, talent, and brain power to make Houston better. Houston will only remain an international city that can compete on a global scale if, and only if, we retain our best and brightest minds.

I also encourage college students and executives to give back to low-income communities. While Houston can boast of its national infrastructure feats like Reliant, Minute Maid, Toyota, the Galleria, and light rail, our city has some of the poorest African American communities with crumbling, aged infrastructure dating back to the 1960s. Elected leaders will need your brain power and expertise to rebuild these communities both physically and socially.

As I prepare to leave and allow you to return back to your learning experience, I feel obligated to say this to you. We also need people who have careers in science, engineering, and technology to run for office. In most cases, elected leaders establish policies and provide government funding for major research and development projects that will improve the quality of life for all Americans. It was President Kennedy who provided the funding and set the policy that America would put a man on the moon in the twentieth century. It was the minds of our great scientist and engineers at NASA that made it actually happen. As a policymaker with a background in science and engineering, you will have an advantage in ensuring that our policies prepare our cities and states to innovate and compete in the new global technology-driven economy.

As Malcolm said, "the future belongs to those who prepare for it today."

Repeat after me: today I take responsibility for my success!

Thank you for allowing me to share in your learning experience this morning. May God bless you to be the best "you" that you can be.

Informative

The purpose of an informative speech is to define and explain a specific topic that is relevant to your audience. Informative speeches are inherently definitional and explanatory in nature because your objective is to teach the audience something new and interesting. You must have clear objectives to determine your expected outcome(s) in advance. If you are giving an informative speech about the powers of the Office of the Mayor in your city, your outline objectives could be:

1. Identify and explain the legal (City Charter) document that gives the Mayor authority to execute the business of the municipality.

2. Identify and explain the Mayor's legislative authority and how the public policy process works.

3. Identify and explain the Mayor's budgetary authority and responsibility to pass a balanced budget.

These are clear outline objectives that will provide a framework for formulating a speech to inform your audience of the legal, legislative, and budgetary power of the Mayor in your city. An informative speech should be clear and concise in its purpose. The audience should take away specific knowledge about a particular subject matter.

Persuasive

The purpose of a persuasive speech is to motivate and convince your audience to adopt certain beliefs and/or take a specific course of action. President Barack Obama illustrated this concept best when he led a massive campaign to sell health care reform legislation to his colleagues in Congress and the American people. His persuasive argument to Congress was for a "yes" vote, but his argument to the American people was for a favorable "public opinion" vote. Below is President Barack Obama's persuasive speech on health care reform to a joint session of Congress.

Madam Speaker, Vice President Biden, members of Congress, and the American people:

When I spoke here last winter, this nation was facing the worst economic crisis since the Great Depression. We were losing an average of 700,000 jobs per month. Credit was frozen. And our financial system was on the verge of collapse.

As any American who is still looking for work or a way to pay their bills will tell you, we are by no means out of the woods. A full and vibrant recovery is still many months away. And I will not let up until those Americans who seek jobs can find them -- (applause) -- until those businesses that seek capital and credit can thrive; until all responsible homeowners can stay in their homes. That is our ultimate goal. But thanks to the bold and decisive action we've taken since January, I can stand here with confidence and say that we have pulled this economy back from the brink. (Applause.)

I want to thank the members of this body for your efforts and your support in these last several months, and especially those who've taken the difficult votes that have put us on a path to recovery. I also want to thank the American people for their patience and resolve during this trying time for our nation.

But we did not come here just to clean up crises. We came here to build a future. (Applause.) So tonight, I return to speak to all of you about an issue that is central to that future -- and that is the issue of health care.

I am not the first President to take up this cause, but I am determined to be the last. (Applause.) It has now been nearly a century since Theodore Roosevelt first called for health care reform. In addition, ever since, nearly every President and Congress, whether Democrat or Republican, has attempted to meet this challenge in some way. A bill for comprehensive health reform was first introduced by John Dingell Sr. in 1943. Sixty-five years later, his son continues to introduce that same bill at the beginning of each session. (Applause.)

Our collective failure to meet this challenge -- year after year, decade after decade -- has led us to the breaking point. Everyone understands the extraordinary hardships that are placed on the uninsured, who live every day just one accident or illness away from bankruptcy. These are not primarily people on welfare. These are middle-class Americans. Some can't get insurance on the job. Others are self-employed, and can't afford it, since buying insurance on your own costs you three times as much as the coverage you get from your employer. Many other Americans who are willing and able to pay are still denied insurance due to previous illnesses or conditions that insurance companies decide are too risky or too expensive to cover.

We are the only democracy -- the only advanced democracy on Earth -- the only wealthy nation -- that allows such hardship for millions of its people. There are now more than 30 million American citizens who cannot get coverage. In just a two-year period, one in every three Americans goes without health care coverage at some point. And every day, 14,000 Americans lose their coverage. In other words, it can happen to anyone.

But the problem that plagues the health care system is not just a problem for the uninsured. Those who do have insurance have never had less security and stability than they do today. More and more Americans worry that if you move, lose your job, or change your job, you'll lose your health insurance, too. More and more Americans pay their premiums, only to discover that their insurance company has dropped their coverage when they get sick, or won't pay the full cost of care. It happens every day.

One man from Illinois lost his coverage in the middle of chemotherapy because his insurer found that he hadn't reported gallstones that he didn't even know about. They delayed his treatment, and he died because of it. Another woman from Texas was about to get a double mastectomy when her insurance company canceled her policy because she forgot to declare a case of acne. By the time she had her insurance reinstated, her breast cancer had more than doubled in size. That is heartbreaking, it is wrong, and no one should be treated that way in the United States of America. (Applause.)

Then there's the problem of rising cost. We spend one and a half times more per person on health care than *any other country, but we aren't any healthier for it. This is one of the reasons that insurance premiums have gone up three times faster than wages. It's why so many employers -- especially small businesses -- are forcing their employees to pay more for insurance, or are dropping their coverage entirely. It's why so many aspiring entrepreneurs cannot afford to open a business in the first place, and why American businesses that compete internationally -- like our automakers -- are at a huge disadvantage. And it's why those of us with health insurance are also paying a hidden and growing tax for those without it -- about $1,000 per year that pays for somebody else's emergency room and charitable care.*

Finally, our health care system is placing an unsustainable burden on taxpayers. When health care costs grow at the rate they have, it puts greater pressure on programs like Medicare and Medicaid. If we do nothing to slow these skyrocketing costs, we will eventually be spending more on Medicare and Medicaid than every other government program combined. Put simply, our health care problem is our deficit problem. Nothing else even comes close. Nothing else. (Applause.)

Now, these are the facts. Nobody disputes them. We know we must reform this system. The question is how.

There are those on the left who believe that the only way to fix the system is through a single-payer system like Canada's — (applause) -- where we would severely restrict the private insurance market and have the government provide coverage for everybody. On the right, there are those who argue that we should end employer-based systems and leave individuals to buy health insurance on their own.

I've said -- I have to say that there are arguments to be made for both these approaches. However, either one would represent a radical shift that would disrupt the health care most people currently have. Since health care represents one-sixth of our economy, I believe it makes more sense to build on what works and fix what doesn't, rather than try to build an entirely new system from scratch. (Applause.) And that is precisely what those of you in Congress have tried to do over the past several months.

During that time, we've seen Washington at its best and at its worst.

We've seen many in this chamber work tirelessly for the better part of this year to offer thoughtful ideas about how to achieve reform. Of the five committees asked to develop bills, four have completed their work, and the Senate Finance Committee announced today that it will move forward next week. That has never happened before. Our overall efforts have been supported by an unprecedented coalition of doctors and nurses, hospitals, seniors' groups, and even drug companies — many of whom opposed reform in the past. And there is agreement in this chamber on about 80 percent of what needs to be done, putting us closer to the goal of reform than we have ever been.

But what we've also seen in these last months is the same partisan spectacle that only hardens the disdain many Americans have towards their own government.

Instead of honest debate, we've seen scare tactics. Some have dug into unyielding ideological camps that offer no hope of compromise. Too many have used this as an opportunity to score short-term political points, even if it robs the country of our opportunity to solve a long-term challenge. And out of this blizzard of charges and counter-charges, confusion has reigned.

Well, the time for bickering is over. The time for games has passed. (Applause.) Now is the season for action. Now is when we must bring the best ideas of both parties together, and show the American people that we can still do what we were sent here to do. Now is the time to deliver on health care. Now is the time to deliver on health care.

The President's persuasive strategy in the speech is to advocate favorable public opinion themes like security, stability, and fiscal responsibility (deficit reduction) to frame the health care debate. As it relates to the theme of fiscal responsibility (deficit reduction), the President is advancing the claim that our economy and its long-term economic recovery and stability are inextricably tied to a sustainable, cost-efficient health care system. President Obama's purpose for linking health care reform legislation to the economy was to demonstrate:

1. The huge economic implications for the United States federal budget if we do nothing, and

2. That his brand of health care reform would provide fundamental economic structural changes, with long-term benefits, to the American taxpayer.

When Reagan talked about tax policy, he often framed it in the form of job creation and economic stimulus. Consider the following quote from one of his speeches: "Entrepreneurs and their small enterprises are responsible for almost all the economic growth in the United States." This statement was made within the context of a tax policy speech, but he didn't try to explain the complexities of the tax code. Reagan used simple understandable themes that ordinary people could understand. When it came to tax policy and trade, Reagan always framed these complex issues by using themes like entrepreneurialism and economic growth.

So what is the lesson here? Successful speakers delivering a persuasive speech know how to frame issues and connect them to simple, understandable themes that everyone can understand. I call this the **thematic principle.**

We might not understand the intricacies of insurance contracts and public health law, but most of us know what security and stability mean within the context of not being dropped by our insurance company if diagnosed with cancer. We might not understand complex tax policy, but we can agree that entrepreneurialism and economic growth are well-known themes often used when telling the American story.

The **"thematic principle"** has been used by great speechwriters and speakers for centuries. Now you can apply this principle with clarity when preparing for your next public presentation. In order to develop this skill, I encourage you to study great speakers like Abraham Lincoln, Dr. Martin Luther King, Jr., President John F. Kennedy, and Dr. Thomas F. Freeman. Your task is to identify the central themes embedded in their speeches.

Once you hone this skill, you will be able to prepare your own presentation(s) with a sort of panoramic clarity that will keep your speech focused on its purpose. In fact, when you read the newspaper, especially the editorial section, look for the stated and unstated themes of the author. Learning this skill, especially for students, is essential to your development as a proficient writer and speaker.

Exercise: Reread President Obama's health care speech, and see if you can find more themes and write them down.

Strategies for keeping the attention of your audience

Now that you have the attention of your audience, you must keep it! If you start good but lose the attention of your audience midway through your presentation, you run the risk of your entire presentation being forgotten, and you will be written off as a poor speaker.

Law in Action

Listed below are some strategies to help you keep the attention of your audience.

1. Use visual aids to improve retention and keep the attention of your audience.

   Application: *If you are giving a speech on homelessness, showing a dramatic video clip of homeless children living on the streets midway through your presentation will definitely recapture the attention of your audience. Other visual aids may consist of oversized pictures, PowerPoint slides,* *flip charts, overhead projectors, guided handouts, and objects.*

2. Make sure you have clear, short, and concise points. ***Application:*** What are the three successful S's of public speaking?

   a. Stand up to be seen!
   b. Speak up to be heard!
   c. Shut up to be appreciated!

3. Make clear transitional statements for speech continuity. ***Application:*** *"....this leads me to my second point, which clearly explains in detail why so many teens are dropping out of school." You must give your audience a clear indictor that you are moving from one point to the next. For poetic speakers like Doc, transitions are strategically integrated, often by using information from one point as a lead in for the next. (See illustration below in comments on Dr. Freeman's eulogy of Barbara Jordan.)*

4. Remember to interact with your audience. ***Application:*** *You may ask a member of the audience to come to the front to help you demonstrate a point, or you may ask the entire audience to engage in an audience participation exercise. Another tactic politicians use to create energy and get the crowd fired up is the **"call and response"** tactic. Former President Bill Clinton used this tactic in his 1996 speech to the Democratic National Convention. See excerpts of President Clinton's speech, below.*

Now, our opponents have put forward a very different plan -- a risky $550 billion tax scheme *that will force them to ask for even bigger cuts in Medicare, Medicaid, education and the environment than they passed and I vetoed last year.*

But even then, they will not cover the cost of their scheme. So that even then this plan will explode the deficit, which will increase interest rates — by two percent according to their own estimates last year. It will require huge cuts in the very investments we need to grow and to grow together, and at the same time, slow down the economy. You know what higher interest rates mean. To you it means a higher mortgage payment, a higher car payment, a higher credit card payment. To our economy it means businesspeople will not borrow as much money, invest as much money, create as many new jobs, create as much wealth, raise as many raises.

CLINTON: *Do we really want to make that same mistake all over again?*

CROWD: *No.*

CLINTON: *Do we really want to stop economic growth again?*

CROWD: *No.*

CLINTON: *Do we really want to start piling up another mountain of debt?*

CROWD: *No.*

CLINTON: *Do we want to bring back the recession of 1991 and 1992?*

CROWD: *No.*

CLINTON: *Do we want to weaken our bridge to the twenty-first century?*

CROWD: *No.*

CLINTON: *Of course, we don't. We have an obligation, you and I, to leave our children a legacy of opportunity, not a legacy of debt. Our budget would be balanced today -- we would have a surplus today -- if we didn't have to make the interest payments on the debt run up in the 12 years before the Clinton-Gore Administration took office. Thank you.*

Note: The **"call and response"** tactic works well when there are large passionate crowds that agree with your point of view.

5.   Use voice inflection. ***Application:*** *As I previously stated, Doc would take his audience on a journey with the roller-coaster tones and pitches he masterfully used during his presentation. You must learn how to project your voice to fill the empty spaces of the room. Your voice is the tool you use to seduce your audience into submission.*

As I conclude this law, it is imperative that you understand that your delivery is considered game time. You don't begin to prepare for a game on the day of the game. You must perfect your delivery behind closed doors. Once you are sure that your content is the right message for the right audience, you must give a clear, concise, and powerful delivery to connect with your audience. That's what public speaking is all about—Making a Human Connection.

CASE STUDY

Eulogy of the late Congresswoman Barbara Jordan

January 20, 1996

By Dr. Thomas F. Freeman

When I last saw Barbara it was at a Martin Luther King concert by the Chicago Sinfonietta conducted by Paul Freeman, where Barbara said, as the narrator following the introduction, "I am pleased to be here not only with Tom's (Doc) brother Paul but just to hear Tom introduce me. In fact, I always like to hear him introduce me because he always makes me feel as though I am somebody." It was not necessary to make Barbara feel like somebody—she was somebody!

[Comment] Notice that Doc did not begin with a conventional introduction, acknowledging dignitaries. He began with a memorable story of his former student, showing his personal connection with a national figure that most people only knew publicly. Doc's introduction-- a reminiscent story of his last encounter with Barbara-- visibly stirred the emotions of the audience, but most importantly, it got their attention!

When she appeared on campus at the forensic tournament named after her, she said, "The one thing I shall never be able to forgive Tom for is inflicting on me a pattern of speech which I have not been able to eradicate." She did her teacher an honor when she went on further to say, "but when I return to Washington I shall recommend to President Jimmy Carter that he spend three weeks with Tom Freeman. And I guarantee that he will not be the same thereafter."

[Comment] Notice that Doc continues by telling a second story to further impress upon the minds of the mourners that his special relationship with Barbara, as her mentor and teacher, did not end when she graduated

117

from Texas Southern University. I believe Doc wanted to show the value of mentor/mentee relationships in education and, in particular, how his relationship with Barbara blossomed into a life-long friendship that lasted over forty years, until death separated them. Doc wanted the audience to know that his relationship with Barbara could not be limited to her short time at Texas Southern University.

Not for three weeks but for four years! It was my privilege to assist in the nurture of Barbara in the most plastic years of her life. As teacher, debate coach, counselor, and friend, I had many opportunities to interact with her so that now I have precious memories that will linger with me forever.

[Comment] Notice how Doc strategically integrates his transition from one point to the next. "Not for three weeks but for four years" is the transition sentence that connects and integrates the narrative to create continuity. Speech continuity is a critical factor in determining delivery success. If your transitions are not integrated in an orderly fashion, the continuity of your presentation will be interrupted, possibly causing you to stumble or lose your chain of thought. Speech continuity is the key to memorizing your key points.

She was a student who learned her lesson well. So well that without my further tutelage she catapulted into national eminence. On this day, when so many have gathered to pay tribute to this great lady, indulge me as I share the emotion of Mark Anthony at the funeral of Julius Caesar.

[Comment] Here you will see Doc setting up his closing by utilizing the emotion of a well-known personality from history (Mark Anthony). Utilizing well-known personalities from history is an effective communication tactic: people who are familiar with the story will have a frame of reference for how the speaker really feels, and people who are not familiar with the story will listen closely so that they can research this unfamiliar story that most people seem to know and appreciate. This is what I call the poetic closing.

Friends, Romans, and countrymen, lend me your ears; I come

118

here to speak at Caesar's funeral. He was my friend, faithful and true to me. I speak not to disprove what Brutus spoke. I speak here only what I know. Bear with me; my heart is there in the coffin with Barbara. I must pause and let it come back to me. Barbara! Barbara! Barbara!

We thank you for just being Barbara!

[Comment] As Doc ends his remarks with the poetic closing, he strategically finds a way to connect the story to the gravity of the occasion. If you are going to use a poetic closing, you must make sure your poetry connects with the reality and context of the occasion, or people will wonder why you told that story or recited that poem.

LAW V
KNOW WHEN TO SHUT UP

LAW V

KNOW WHEN TO SHUT UP

> "The ending is everything. Plan all the way to it, taking into account all the possible consequences, obstacles, and twists of fortune that might reverse your hard work."
> **Robert Green**

LAW DEFINED

The skillful art of knowing when and how to conclude your presentation.

PRINCIPLE
Always End Things Well

Don't Kill Your Audience

The best visual that comes to mind when I think about this principle takes me back in time to the experience of the Apostle Paul. The scriptures reveal that Paul preached so long that a man fell asleep, fell out of the window, broke his neck, and died. The lesson: Don't kill your audience with too much rhetoric! If you know anything about the writings of the Apostle Paul, you know he was a very knowledgeable scholar who wrote masterpieces (letters) concerning the doctrine of Jesus Christ. However, no matter how valuable your information, you must know when to shut up. Even a great presentation can become disastrous if the speaker doesn't know when and/or how to end it. Dr. Freeman has one of the most unique closing styles I have ever witnessed from a speaker. He knows how to leave you "wanting more," as he concludes his speech with a climactic finish that propels you to a suspended height of consciousness. Dr. Freeman is a scholar of scholars with years of experience and knowledge to share with his listeners, but he knows when and how to end his presentation, which results in his audience thirsting for more. Simply stated, he knows when to shut up, and so should you. I know you are bursting with knowledge and passion and want to get it all out. However, you must judge the disposition of your listening audience and be able to ascertain if you are killing them with too much rhetoric.

LAW IN ACTION

Listed below are several audience feedback responses that let you know it's time to shut up!

1. When you hear constant sighing by several members of the audience, *it's time to shut up!*

2. When you see constant fidgeting by several members of your audience, *it's time to shut up!*

3. When you see several audience members tapping on the table with an uninterested look, *it's time to shut up!*

4. When multiple people start walking out, *it's time to shut up!*

5. When you see a sea of irritated facial expressions, *it's time to shut up!*

6. In most cases, if you have been speaking longer than 30 minutes, *it's time to shut up!*

It doesn't take an hour and thirty minutes to say what you could've said in just thirty minutes. You can give a great presentation in thirty minutes or less, i.e. Dr. Martin Luther King's historic "I Have a Dream" speech. The only disclaimer I have to this rule is the fact that you may be asked to speak before hostile crowds that will never agree with you no matter what you say. For example, when President Barack Obama spoke to a room full of Republicans on national TV about supporting his then pending Health Care Reform Bill, he got constant sighs, fidgeting, taps, and irritated facial expressions during his presentation. In a format like this, you must hold your ground, say what you have to say, and vigorously defend your position.

Always End Things Well

The principle of always "ending things well" is not only a public-speaking principle, but also, a life principle. Can you imagine being a law abiding citizen your entire life and suddenly deciding at the age of 75 to pursue a life of crime? Can you imagine an employee working for a company for 20 years, and on the day of his "going away" party, he gets caught stealing and loses his retirement benefits and good name? Sounds absolutely absurd, right? Wouldn't this infuriate you if one of your loved ones did this? Wouldn't you say, "What in the world were you thinking?" The reason I am giving such extreme examples is because my point is extreme: don't destroy a great presentation because you don't know when and how to SHUT UP! Your closing must be tactful, strategic, and artful, which takes careful planning and execution. Most preachers are familiar with this concept as they try to take you on a journey and end with the perfect climactic closing to put the entire presentation into perspective.

Have you ever watched a great movie that had a terrible ending? I can't speak for you, but when this happened to me, I felt an overwhelming since of disappointment because I had expected a strong finale that would leave an indelible impression on my mind. Just as important as it is to get your audience's attention in the beginning, it is equally important to focus their attention, once again, by leaving them with a well-orchestrated closing that they will remember.

Listed on the following pages are specific closing strategies and tactics.

THE ART OF THE CLOSING

The Summary Closing

The summary closing is often used to reiterate key main points that help the speaker accomplish his/her purpose of the presentation. Just because the points are clear in your mind doesn't mean they are clear to the audience. Consider an excerpt from Dale Carnegie's book, *Public Speaking for Success.*[1] The speaker is a woman who is enlisting support for a fund-raising "walkathon" for breast cancer research.

> *In short, ladies and gentleman, the statistics I have presented to you prove that the number of women being diagnosed with breast cancer is increasing every year. Much has been learned already to alleviate their pain and suffering, but there is so much more we must learn. Our research is making significant breakthroughs, but we have much more to do. Your help, by joining our walkathon next week, will help increase the funds needed for this important cause.*

Can you see what the speaker has done? By using the summary technique, she has summed up the purpose of the speech in one succinct summary paragraph. This particular summary gives you the key points in the speech while transitioning to a call for action, which leads me to the next closing technique.

The Call-to-Action Closing

If you are giving a presentation that requires your audience to take specific action, then you must be clear and concise in

125

communicating the four Ws:

Why: If you are giving a speech that is persuasive in nature and will require some action on the part of your audience, you must be clear and concise about how their individual contributions will have a direct impact in helping to fulfill the vision you articulated during the presentation. In the aforementioned excerpt, the speaker did a great job of communicating why audience members should participate in the walkathon benefiting breast cancer research. She presented evidence of a growing problem, what's currently being done, and how their support would advance groundbreaking research to solve a problem that could one day affect them.

When Doc spoke with new recruits about joining the team, he made it a point to clearly articulate how our individual performances would play a key role in continuing the phenomenal legacy of the TSU Debate Team. I left my first meeting with a sense of connection to a great legacy and a personal responsibility to use my gifts and talents to be a part of something much bigger than me.

What: When there is a call to action, always be specific about what you are asking your audience to do. For example, the speaker who spoke about breast cancer made a specific request for audience members to join the walkathon to raise money for the cause. Always communicate to your audience what actions you want them to take. In a call-to-action closing, always strive to get a committed decision from your audience.

When: Always make sure your audience understands the timing. Opportunities must be put within the context of time. To create a sense of urgency, the breast cancer advocate mentioned that statistics consistently show breast cancer is increasing every year. This lets the audience know that time is of the essence and action is needed now. In the business world, this is why advertisers use the language "for a limited time only." An advertiser understands that a prospect must have an incentive for acting within a certain timeframe. Most people tend to put off making decisions and must be strategically guided to choose, within a specific timeframe, what you are offering.

Where: I'm sure the breast cancer advocate had flyers or some type of literature with the specifics (who, what, when, where) so participants would know where to be on the day of the event. If you are in business, there must be no ambiguity about where to find your products or services. You must make sure the audience gets accurate information with your address, website, and clear language demonstrating the benefits of your products or services.

I should also mention that it is very important to make sure there are no cumbersome processes that would discourage potential customers, recruits, etc. Most sales presenters will have staff available to meet with customers to walk them through the closing process after the presentation. Handouts with instructional details are also an excellent way to communicate specifics to potential customers or recruits.

The Poetic Closing

The poetic closing utilizes literary devices like metaphors, similes, and analogies to create pictorial images of your themes. This tactic transforms words into mental images that will be seared into the consciousness of your audience long after you are gone.

Consider the following excerpt from President Ronald Reagan's last farewell address on January 11, 1989.

> *And that's about all I have to say tonight. Except for one thing. The past few days when I've been at that window upstairs, I've thought a bit of the "shining city upon a hill." The phrase comes from John Winthrop, who wrote it to describe the America he imagined. What he imagined was important because he was an early Pilgrim, an early freedom man. He journeyed here on what today we'd call a little wooden boat; and like the other Pilgrims, he was looking for a home that would be free.*

> *I've spoken of the shining city all my political life, but I don't know if I ever quite communicated what I saw when I said it. But in my mind it was a tall proud city built on rocks stronger than oceans, wind-swept, God-blessed, and teeming with people of all kinds living in harmony and peace, a city with free ports that hummed with commerce and creativity, and if there had to be city walls, the walls had doors and the doors were open to anyone with the will and the heart to get here. That's how I saw it and see it still.*

Notice how President Reagan tactfully used the metaphoric language "city walls with doors" to paint a picture of the theme—opportunity.

The Climax Closing

As a preacher, I am very acquainted with this type of closing. The idea is to close your presentation with clarity and a climactic burst of energy that leaves your audience with information as well as inspiration. Consider Dr. King's closing of his famous "I Have a Dream" speech, which is a collage of the poetic and climatic closings:

> And if America is to be a great nation, this must become true. So let freedom ring from the prodigious hilltops of New Hampshire. Let freedom ring from the mighty mountains of New York.
>
> Let freedom ring from the heightening Alleghenies of Pennsylvania.
>
> Let freedom ring from the snow-capped Rockies of Colorado.
>
> Let freedom ring from the curvaceous peaks of California.
>
> But not only that, let freedom, ring from Stone Mountain of Georgia.
>
> Let freedom ring from Lookout Mountain of Tennessee.

Let freedom ring from every hill and molehill of Mississippi.

From every mountainside, let freedom ring.

When we let freedom ring, when we let it ring from every village and every hamlet, from every state and every city, we will be able to speed up that day when all of God's children, black men and white men, Jews and Gentiles, Protestants and Catholics, will be able to join hands and sing in the words of the old Negro spiritual, "Free at last, free at last. Thank God Almighty, we are free at last."

When Dr. King finished, the crowd erupted into a thunderous applause, demonstrating their level of inspiration and buy-in of the message. This speech had a purpose and that **purpose was to galvanize the masses in a public display of support to influence civil rights legislation.** Dr. King's speech could not be a dull, informative speech about public policy but had to be inspirational and persuasive in its objectives. The climactic method of closing is best used when there are large crowds that will feed off your energy and will create an atmosphere of inspiration for action. Presidential candidate Barack Obama mastered this technique when he was running for office. He would often end his campaign speeches with a lofty climactic closing that left the audience fired up and "ready to vote."

Leave them wanting more.

In the beginning of this book, I said I wanted to help you find your voice. Doc helped me find my voice by teaching me how to:

1. Master My Mental Self (Law I).

2. Prepare With Discipline (Law II).

3. Speak Before I Speak (Law III).

4. Speak When I Speak (Law IV).

5. Know When to Shut Up! (Law V).

While this book contains some of the core principles I learned as a member of Doc's Debate team, there is much more I could say about the science and art of public speaking. However, Law 5 explicitly states, "Know When to Shut Up," and that's exactly what I'm going to do by ending this book now. Thank you for giving me your time and attention to learn *Public Speaking the Freeman Way.*

THE GREAT DEBATERS WORKSHOP AT TEXAS SOUTHERN UNIVERSITY

Dr. Freeman with renowned actor Denzel Washington.

The Great Debaters *actors training under the direction of*
Dr. Freeman.

The Great Debaters *filming on the campus of Texas Southern University.*

Texas Southern University Debate Team students with The Great Debaters *actors.*

DR. THOMAS FREEMAN & AUTHOR PREVIN JONES

My graduation from Texas Southern University, 1999.

Dr. Thomas F. Freeman Day in the City of Houston, City Hall 2009.

ENDNOTES

LAW I

1. John Assaraf. (2008). *The Answer: Grow any business, Achieve financial freedom, and live an extraordinary life. New York:* Atria.

LAW II

1. *The Brain.* History: A&E Home Video. (2009). The brain. [DVD].
2. Ibid.
3. Ibid.
4. Ibid.
5. Sarah Novotny and Len Kravitz, Ph.D.. (2009). The science of breathing. Retrieved March 4, 2010 from http://www.unm.edu/~lkravitz/Article%20folder/Breathing.html

LAW III

1. Granada International. (2008). *Secrets of body language.* History: A&E Television Networks. [DVD].
2. Stephen Lucas. (2007). *The art of public speaking* (9th ed.). New York: McGraw Hill. 313.
3. Nick Morgan. (2000). How to become an authentic speaker. *Harvard Business Review, 86*(1), 115-119.
4. Ann Beall. (2004). Body language speaks: Reading and responding more effectively to hidden communication. *Communication World 21*(2): 18.
5. Richard M. Perloff. (2003). *The dynamics of persuasion: Communication and attitude in the 21st century* (2nd ed.). Mahwah, NJ: Erlbaum. 170-174.

LAW IV

1. Encyclopedia Britannica, Inc., Retrieved February 28, 2011, from http://dictionary.reference.com/browse/diction.
2. Lucas. (2007). The art of public speaking (9th ed.). New York: McGraw Hill. 470.

LAW V

1. Arthur Pell. (2005). *Public speaking for success: Dale Carnegie.* New York: Penguin. 252.